THE **ART** OF *Healing* TRAUMA

Finding Joy through Creativity,

Spirituality, and Forgiveness

ALISON PERRY-DAVIES

in·fluence

PARTNERS IN PUBLISHING

Published by Influence Publishing Inc.
in partnership with Ali Way Art Publishing, October 2021
ISBN: 978-1-7778830-0-3

Editor: Danielle Anderson
Cover Painting: Alison Perry-Davies
Book and Cover Design: Tara Eymundson
Proofreader: Lee Robinson

Dedication

To my daughter Jessica—Jessie Doodle—thank you for allowing me to share your story, our story. You are the bravest, wisest, strongest woman I know, and I love you and I am honoured to be your mum.

Thank you to Ryan, my cute, little baby-boy son, for trusting me. You are an amazing man, and my heart is full to overflow with love for you and Lauren and Hannah and Kashus.

To Hannah, my late night deep conversations exploring all things wild and wonderful together forever granddaughter, thank you; I am a better person because you are in my life.

To Kashus, my always curious, lover of stories and alternate theories grandson, thank you for always helping me to see the world through the eyes of science and endless possibilities.

To David, my closest friend, my biggest cheerleader, my lover, my husband, my partner and love of my life, thank you for being you and letting me be me. I adore you.

Thank you Dave and Jess for knowing you could not speak or even make a sound when I was in that zone, and you were so gracious and generous about it all.

Thank you my beautiful Sammie, our German Shepherd; I owe you so many long walks.

Thank you to my beautiful family, near and far; I love you all so much.

Thank you to my friends to whom I didn't return calls and texts as I was pouring myself into this book, and you loved me anyways. Thank you for encouraging me along the way.

To every person who helped me and encouraged me and believed in me and told me it was going to be okay all those times I could not see that for myself, thank you.

Thank you so much to those who took the time to read my book and give me testimonials, your encouragement and support mean so much;
Francis Dick, Gwen Rowe, Janelle Breese Biagioni, Rik Leaf, and Dr. Marion Ehrenberg.

Thank you to the amazing team of Influence Publishing,
Anita and Tara and Lee and Danielle and Marilyn and Julie, our wonderful, magical, marvelous Julie, who pulled a story out of me I didn't know I had.

And now to you dear reader, whether I know you or don't know you, know this: my heart is for you, always. My desire in writing this book is that even one person—a person who, like me, didn't see a way out—will find hope and inspiration and their own way to a life of balance and love and joy. I hope you keep creating; it really is the art of healing trauma. Peace.

Testimonials

"Ali's story is raw and captivating. I had a visceral response as I turned each page of her book. A life of tragedy that shakes you to your core and then inspires anyone who dares to follow her journey of self-discovery. An amazing, fearless, inspiring, beautiful woman warrior who selflessly becomes an open book. Thank you, Ali, for your courage, tenacity, brilliance, creativity, humour, for you truly are a bringer of light, love, and healing."

Francis Dick, Kwakwaka'wakw artist

"In her book *The Art of Healing Trauma*, author Ali Perry-Davies bravely shares her personal experiences with trauma. For readers who themselves are survivors of trauma, they may find support and validation in these authentic accounts. However, *The Art of Healing Trauma* is so much more than that. Based on the author's life-long learning, including study and front-line work with trauma survivors, she shows how creative expression may offer a path to healing. The book is filled with insights and suggestions for engaging in this creative healing process that may be useful to trauma survivors as well as therapists who are looking at fresh approaches to supporting their clients."

Marion F. Ehrenberg, Ph.D., Psychologist

"Ali invites readers into her world with a gentle warmth—much like inviting a neighbour in for a cup of tea. Her story demonstrates the complexity of life with loss, life with trauma, life with brain injury, and how one navigates unpredictable, life-altering experiences. Ali brilliantly weaves threads of creativity, courage, love, honesty, forgiveness, and most important of all, healing, through her story. This book will lead others to their path of healing through creativity—a true gift."

Janelle Breese Biagioni, RPC, MPCC-s
CEO, CGB Centre for Traumatic Life Losses

"The Art of Healing Trauma" is a courageously and uncompromisingly written first-hand testimony, as Ali Perry-Davies takes readers on her journey of overcoming life's darkest hours. This book will be an inspiration for those who are walking their own dark night of the soul and need encouragement to believe there is a light at the end of the tunnel and that it is worth every step. Highly recommend!"

Rik Leaf, Singer/Songwriter, Producer, Author of *Four Homeless Millionaires*

"Ali courageously, and against all odds, brightly shines light on the darkness with honest vulnerability and love. A true wisdom keeper and storyteller, she takes you along on her inspiring journey to healing. Her strength and authenticity will resonate deeply and touch your heart like it has mine."

Gwen Rowe, Heart and Sole Wellness

Contents

The View from Where I Stand: An Introduction of Sorts

"I needed to write, to express myself through written language not only so that others might hear me but so that I could hear myself."
Gabor Maté, *In the Realm of Hungry Ghosts: Close Encounters with Addiction*

O ne day, when I was around fifteen years old, I found myself walking down Blue Mountain Avenue in Coquitlam and wondering if I would ever be free of feeling utterly alone and detached from the world. I remember thinking that even the leaves on the trees didn't look right. Everything seemed so distorted, like I was in some kind of poorly filmed low-budget movie.

It would take me many years of feeling lost to comprehend the depth of the impact that trauma was having on my life, and on my body. I didn't yet know that my amygdala was stuck in high alert, perceiving threats at every turn. I didn't understand that my hippocampus was now underactive due to my brain's response to stress, impacting my memory and my ability to process these traumatic events or the feelings that arose from them. I didn't recognize that trauma was putting my entire body, mind, and spirit in a constant state of fight or flight, and since I had no ability to do either, it just remained in that state—constantly warning, constantly reacting, with no relief.

INTRODUCTION

I didn't know then how hiding my trauma could make me physically, emotionally, mentally, and spiritually unwell. I was just a mixed-up, terrified kid, and all I knew was that I had to make sure no one ever found out my secrets.

Walking through life with trauma is much like walking through life with a sprained ankle. At first the ankle is swollen and sore, and it is difficult to find a position that will ease the pain. Over time, the pain decreases and the injury disappears from your daily thoughts. Then, just when you think it is healed, it starts to ache again out of nowhere—or worse yet, there is a slight turn of the ankle and it feels like it has been torn all over again. My life was much like that ankle. I put myself and others through a lot over the years while I flailed around, trying to hold my life in a way that didn't hurt. As time passed, I first found many things to distract me, and eventually I discovered ways to bring healing and wholeness. Now, I want to share some of what I have learned.

My ongoing healing has been (and continues to be) a journey rather than a destination. I know that to some of you, that phrase might seem like some cheesy bumper sticker phrase, an empty platitude. To others, the thought of healing being drawn out over an extended period of time might not seem good enough. I get it. Oh, do I ever get that when we want some freedom in our lives, the last thing we want to hear is how this all just takes time. Unfortunately, for me, that's the truth. It took time, peeling back layer after layer, taking one shaky little step after the other.

I started this book thinking I would be writing about forgiveness and the healing that it brings, and there are stories of forgiveness throughout here for sure. As I continued to write, though, it became clear to me that all of the different paths and experiences throughout my life had created a kaleidoscope of healing. It was never about one prayer, one hurt to forgive, one sacred moment, one counselling session, one prescription, diet, exercise regime, close friend, religious experience, path of enlightenment, psychic reading, prophetic word, course or courses or studies in specific fields. It wasn't a day with one big "a-ha" moment, but instead a series of them—of all of them.

This "whole-istic" healing path is not one that can be easily described in a linear fashion. Some layers took years, decades even, to fully unravel, and many of them overlap with one another. So, rather than trying to write this book in a linear fashion, I have taken the messages I want to share and arranged them into four sections. I've started with The Foundations of Trauma, where I talk about how everything began and the impact my trauma has had both on my life and on the lives of others. Next comes A Path to Healing, covering the steps I have taken along my path to recovery. This journey encompasses mind, body, spirit, and emotion—all four of these areas were impacted by trauma, and in order to truly heal, I needed to listen and pay attention to each aspect. Then there is Visions, Whispers, and Knowings—the ways that I learned to trust, see, and listen. Finally, there is Building Community, where I share the stories of friends and family members who have taught me important lessons and inspired me with their own efforts to recover from trauma.

> *"As long as you keep secrets and suppress information, you are fundamentally at war*
>
> *with yourself...The critical issue is allowing yourself to know what you know.*
>
> *That takes an enormous amount of courage."*

— **Bessel A. van der Kolk**, *The Body Keeps the Score: Brain, Mind, and Body in the Healing of Trauma*

As I wrote this book, I was clear on one thing: I did not want to share a long list of traumatic events I had experienced. I want to let you, the reader, know a bit of what I have gone through so that you have an idea of where I have come from, but I was considering leaving some of my experiences out. I didn't want to share sad stories just for the sake of it or to ramble on about the horrible things that have happened to me and the ways I have behaved that sometimes make me cringe when I remember them. Then I talked about these feelings with my friend Gwen, who is a beautiful healer, and she said to me, "Ali, I get that you don't want to focus on the trauma itself, but you just need to remember that if they can see some of where you have come from, that level of honesty and vulnerability about your own despair will bring hope. Tell them like you have told me about the dark days between—that is where they can find their way to believing they can heal too."

I have taken her advice and shared some of these "dark days between"—the days between when my pain began and when my healing began, where hope stays hidden. This was a place where I was still unaware of what was actually happening inside of me. I didn't feel as frightened as much as I felt threatened; I didn't feel angry as much as I felt attacked. I wasn't seeing clearly because I was both overwhelmed with these feelings and yet also completely unaware of them and the impact they were having on my life. Through this, I hope to share with you my very intimate relationship with trauma and pain so that I can show those who find themselves on the same path that they too can find healing.

As you will come to see, creativity has played a huge role in my journey. It has given me hope and allowed me space to find a sense of calm that helped me move forward and discover an even greater level of healing. Painting, photography, and writing poems, stories, and songs have all allowed me to find space in my heart and in my mind—space to catch my breath and try again and again and again. I have placed some of these works throughout the book to give a glimpse of the many ways I have used creativity to process, express, and explore all that is happening in and around me.

My healing has come in waves and whooshes and moments, and each time I find a little more freedom, a little more peace, a little more love. There have been beautiful times and angry times and painful times and sacred times and terrifying times, and all of them have brought me here, to this place and this time. For that, I am grateful. By writing this book, I want to share with you the ways I have "whole-istically" healed my whole being: mind, body, spirit, and emotion.

Through all of this, the message I want to share is really quite simple: that there is hope. There is always hope.

Part 1

The Foundations of Trauma

1

Beautiful Chaos and Other Great Beginnings

"If we carry intergenerational trauma (and we do), then we also carry intergenerational wisdom. It's in our genes and in our DNA."
Kazu Haga

Intergenerational or transgenerational trauma are psychological terms that express how that trauma can be passed down from one generation to the next, not only through parenting but also through our actual DNA. Although this is still a rather new field of research, there is evidence to suggest that this phenomenon is very real. I, for one, am a person who believes in its existence as I have seen the evidence firsthand—both through my clients when I worked as a disability case manager and through my personal experience coming from a long line of intergenerational trauma. This is not to say that I haven't also seen intergenerational wisdom and love and many other beautiful gifts. Sometimes, though, we need to first clear the rubble and heal before we can access all the wonderful things waiting for us.

When my mum was four, her parents divorced. Her biological mother took her sister Glee while her biological father kept her and her brother Billy—at least for a while. One day, her father gave her a box and told her to put her things into it because he couldn't take care of her anymore. She wept and begged him not to send her away, promising she would be a good girl, but it was no use; for whatever reason, he felt he could not keep her. So, she packed up her things in that box, and her father dropped her off with a neighbour. She spent the next year moving from household to household, living with one neighbour and then the next.

I don't want to share too much about Mum's experiences as they were hers, not mine, and she was a very private person. I can only say that she shared with me some abuses that took place throughout her life, and that she was an incredibly strong person with a compassionate heart who did not want anyone to know the unkindness she herself experienced.

One day, a lady came to visit from a small town not far from where Mum was living. She and her husband were unable to have children, and they had heard there was a little girl who needed a home. She asked Mum if she would like to come live with them. Mum told me she asked if they had a piano, and the nice lady said they would get one. And that was that. Mum went to live with the couple, they got a piano, and they eventually adopted her.

Mum never heard anything from her biological mother or her sister Glee. As for her brother, her biological father brought him for a visit once about a year after Mum found her new home. The couple, my grandparents, tried to adopt Billy as well, but Mum's biological father wouldn't allow it. After that, Mum never saw her brother again. Uncle Billy died at only twenty-two as a decorated war hero, losing his life while fighting in the Second World War. Mum missed him until the very end of her life and talked of him often. I hope they had a wonderful reunion on the other side.

Mum lived her life never understanding why she was the one left behind, and even though she mostly spoke of how grateful she was to be raised by the parents she had, I am sure she carried that pain deep inside her throughout her life.

Dad, in contrast, was born into a big family with lots of love; however, they also experienced lots of loss and pain. One of his brothers, Rex, died in a boating accident when Dad was very young, and then a few weeks later his sister Bunny passed away from a congenital heart condition. Dad thought the grief was too much for her. When he and I spent time together in the last year of his life, he often spoke to me about his sister Bunny—how much he loved her, and how losing her was something he never really got over. Another loss came when his dad, my grandpa, died when Dad was eleven years old. At this point, Dad went to live with his older brother Bill and his family.

As one of the younger of thirteen children, Dad lost ten siblings over the course of his life. When his sister Noreen passed away in 2017, I called to see how he was doing. My brother Bruce had passed away the year prior, and I knew the incredible pain that came with this experience. I told Dad that I could not have known how hard it was to lose a sibling until I experienced it myself, and that I couldn't imagine it got any easier with each one you lose. Dad was quiet for a bit, then said, "No, it sure doesn't."

At the time, Dad was in his late eighties and unable to drive from where he lived in Tsawwassen up to Salmon Arm in the interior of British Columbia where the funeral was to be held. I was recovering from a motor vehicle accident at the time and unable to drive, but thankfully my friend Leelee could take us there. I am so grateful that we had that time together and that my dad was able to be with his remaining two brothers as they said goodbye to their sister.

My parents met quite young as they lived in adjoining towns growing up. They married in 1951 and went on to have a big family of their own. I grew up with four brothers: Bruce, Doug, Byron, and Donnie—I was the only girl and a middle child. We lived in a big white house on Rochester Avenue in Coquitlam, British Columbia, in a neighbourhood where kids played all day in the summer, only heading home when the streetlights came on at night. Dad was gone a lot for work as he was in the import and export business, which took him all around the world, so many of my memories from these early days are of my mum and the little things she would do to make life feel like an adventure. I loved that about her. One of my favourite memories was when she would make us "special milk" when we came home from school for lunch, which was milk dressed up with a little sugar, some vanilla, and a dash of food colouring. She would choose a different colour every day, and I remember racing home in anticipation, excited to find out what the colour would be.

As a child, I didn't know how deeply my parents' trauma had impacted them—and all of us, really, as generational trauma does. While I don't remember whether or not my parents seemed close—I don't think it was something I paid attention to at the time—I never saw my parents argue and had no real reason to expect there was a problem. What I couldn't have known as a child was how unhappy my father was in their marriage. He was not the bad guy; there was no bad guy in this story, rather a story that was being kept secret, and he was doing his best to cope and be a good father through it all. I couldn't have known or understood that in the midst of it all, he had fallen in love with someone else. I didn't know how hopeful he must have felt after likely feeling trapped for years. *I didn't know, but my intuition did.*

Since I was a small child, I have had dreams and knowings—whispers of things that had not yet happened or been revealed. When I was seven years old, I was constantly afraid my parents would divorce despite being reassured over and over again that they wouldn't. This was especially odd as it was the sixties, when divorce was not something that was spoken of. Then, one day, I once again sat on my daddy's knee and asked him once again if he and Mum were getting a divorce. And that day he said, "I can't lie to you, princess. Yes, we are."

As I recall, what happened next is that I ran down the stairs and screamed at my mum, telling her it was her fault that Daddy was leaving us. I will never forget the look on her face; it seemed that this was the first she had heard of this. How terrible that must have been for her, especially given her past rejections. This was never how my dad wanted things to go. Generational trauma is always hovering, always finding ways into our lives.

My dad found his true love and happiness, but it came at an enormous cost. He lived with such shame for leaving, and he missed us all. This was a time when there was not a lot of emphasis put on co-parenting or creating spaces for healing, but instead on picking sides and finding fault. How very unfortunate. As a child, or even as a young adult, I really did not understand why he had to leave. Some things just take time to understand. Today, I realize that Dad was a man to whom family meant everything, and I understand how very high the price he paid was.

Trauma, pain, abuse, abandonment, bitterness, fear, anxiety, depression—these words tumble and dance and weave together, one creating the other over and over and over. They fill our minds and our thoughts and our lives until we end up stuck in some sort of hidden world, a place where the rest of humanity seems to be functioning without any knowledge of who we really are. The world is oblivious to the swirling in our minds, the gripping pain in our hearts, the complete inability to hold a thought in place, to trust, to laugh honestly, to love, or to have a moment free of absolute and utter shame.

How did we get here? And more importantly, how do we get out?

My family now included a mum who felt rejected throughout her life, a dad who had lost so much and lived with shame, and my "step" mom Sandy who had her own past hurts. (I am not a fan of the title of stepmom; it seems to lack for me all that she means and has meant to me over my life.) I had a new brother, John, and a new sister, Kim—finally, a sister! Soon two new brothers, Jamie and Michael, would join this marvelous mosaic. Somehow, we all learned to love and forgive and make a family. Things weren't always smooth, and it has taken years for us to blend and mend together. Today I adore my family, all nine of us, and I am so grateful that we have found a way to be who we are. We really do put the "fun" in dysfunctional!

Unfortunately, my parents' divorce and the trauma that came with it was not my only struggle. At the time when I learned my daddy was leaving, I was already being touched in ways little children should never be touched. A life of secrets was already underway.

For those who are sexually abused as a child, the way we see the world becomes skewed. The way we see and think and feel and process is shattered into pieces, often completely without our knowledge. We then go through life with a deep knowing that colours every aspect of our life, unaware of how it is impacting our bodies, minds, perceptions, and actions. We don't trust anyone because we feel that we can't tell a soul about this experience that is so dark and so shameful. We know what happens when we speak, so we figure out pretty early when we shouldn't—or at least, we believe we do. And that lesson is simple: never, ever tell.

There are many reasons people, and specifically children, don't tell others about the abuse they experience. They may be afraid to tell, especially if the abuser has threatened them. Later in my life, as an adult, I did report what happened to me and who the person was to the police. I had the option to move forward with charges and chose not to for a variety of reasons— mostly because having spotted memories of a trauma that happened decades ago can make prosecuting the case difficult, and I did not want to go through that. However, I did all that I could to ensure others would be safe from my abuser at that time.

There may also be a level of confusion—it is difficult to comprehend how someone can hurt you so badly inside and out, especially if you are a child and don't even know what sex is yet. In addition, abusers will often create a reality where the child feels almost a closeness or fondness to them, or at least fosters a bond around a shared secret, and that becomes very puzzling. There can even be physical pleasure during the assault, which can add to the confusion and shame. A body does what a body does, and right and wrong and consent and understanding do not always line up with the physical aspects of what is happening.

A little child who has been touched inappropriately can sometimes have a deep, deep longing for something or someone to help them put the shattered pieces of their world back together. This longing follows them into adolescence and adulthood, and it may express itself as unhealthy relationships with people, food, drugs, money, work, or more. This also puts the person in a place to be abused again in the future, as is what happened to me. I was so afraid to tell anyone anything about what was happening to me, and I don't have an explanation for why. All I know is that I was afraid, so afraid, and I felt shame before I knew what that word even meant. I was swimming in it, drowning in it.

The trauma around the sexual abuse I experienced as a child, teenager, and young adult—first by a family friend and later by strangers—affected how I saw myself and the world around me, creating a pattern that would follow me for many decades. Rape shatters us into so many pieces, and it can take a very long time to find a way to bring together all that has been scattered. There were so many inappropriate ways I accepted treatment, and I sought out love in ALL the wrong places. This set in motion a pattern of self-loathing and shame that would follow me through those "dark days between" and even beyond them, creating a way of seeing and existing in the world that was reckless at times.

One event that demonstrates how trauma manifested in my life happened when my girlfriend Colleen and I were sitting in a car outside of a hotel one night, waiting for our boyfriends who were drinking inside (we were underage, so we could not join them). A guy we had never seen before approached us and started talking to us; eventually, he dared me to come out of the car. Colleen was screaming at me, telling me not to, but I did it anyways. It turns out that this man was a very messed up, angry person. He grabbed me and held a knife to my throat, and for some bizarre reason I began laughing. I think it was partially due to nerves and partially because I thought, *What else could you do to me that hasn't been done? Take your best shot.* He shoved me away and told me I was crazy.

The next morning, we found out that one of our friends was stabbed by that same guy with that same knife later that night and was now paralyzed for life. I was just fifteen years old, and the impact of trauma had already created a way of thinking and being that was so unhealthy and unsafe.

There were many more times when I took chances I shouldn't have and found dangerous situations funny. Laughing became a way to feel some kind of control over the pain. I have been held captive, terrified and unable to escape. I was also beaten to unconsciousness one night. These things convinced me to find ways to meet violence with violence; I didn't want to feel weak or vulnerable.

I was also shot at a few times, albeit one of those times was kind of a funny experience. My girlfriend and I were out with our boyfriends, and her boyfriend was pretty drunk—well, we all were. They were fighting, and eventually he grabbed his rifle. My friend and I ran outside and hid behind a bush while he shot at us. My boyfriend came and told us how stupid we were being—hiding behind a bush as if a bullet wouldn't go through it—then went and took the rifle away from our friend. I don't recall what happened next; likely, we continued drinking together. I understand that it might sound like this situation was completely out of control, and I guess it was, but it was just the lifestyle I was living at the time.

I have memories that I wish I could turn back the clock and change how I behaved—times when I was aggressive and angry and sometimes even violent. These times would come when I felt someone had hurt a person I cared about, and I would physically attack the people I felt were responsible. I even went so far as to take boxing lessons as I felt somehow responsible for protecting the people who were close to me and punishing those who I felt deserved punishing. I am not going to write a long list of stories of people I lost it on. I will just say that I was full of rage, so full of rage, and I had little tolerance for anyone I deemed to be a problem to my friends or my children, nor did I stop to think about the consequences. I am so grateful that in the midst of it all, I had a rule that my children should not be hit—my violence was never directed at them, although my son jokes with me that he was basically grounded non-stop from the age of twelve to sixteen, and a spanking would have been an easier punishment.

I understand now that anger is not actually a root or base emotion. It comes out of fear, and that was something I knew all too well.

Trauma—the day or days we became a victim of abuse or had an experience that changed us—has a way of filtering down through every aspect of our lives. There are many ways we can become traumatized, including abandonment, physical or sexual abuse, bullying and other emotionally abusive events, ritual/religious trauma, and so on. And we now know that although trauma can come from a single event, it more often comes from a series of events over time. Each one leaves a film, a layer, a presence of that person or situation that we carry into every job, relationship, conversation, and meeting. They are still abusing and traumatizing us, showing us that they have the power. We might feel that we have no voice, and until we find ways to quiet the bully in our head, we have no choice but to listen to it.

How many promotions have we blown by not even trying for them? Alternatively, how many have we received only to live in fear that someone will discover who we really are and take it away? How many relationships have we been in that were filled with unkindness? How many dollars have we spent? Glasses of wine have we drank? How many times have we judged others, felt judged, hidden from everyone—including ourselves—because who we are is never going to be enough to free us from whatever haunts and taunts us? And most importantly, how do we get out of this place?

I have found that healing from trauma is much like trauma itself: complex and simple all at once. I'm getting ahead of myself, though. First, I learned about young love and consequences and a thing or two about birthing babies.

2

Surprise! A Teenage Mum

"Sometimes the smallest things take up the most room in your heart."
Winnie the Pooh

It was the summer of 1977, and I was laying on the couch one morning when a lump suddenly popped up on my tummy. It terrified me—and this was back in the days before I thought every lump and bump and slight bit of gas or discomfort was probably cancer.

"Muuuuuuuuuum!" I shrilled. Clearly this was a medical anomaly, which meant that Mum could fix it. Mum was a registered nurse (RN), and she could fix anything.

Mum came running, and I lifted my nightie to show her the bump. She put her hands around said lump and did a push here and a prod there, then looked at me and said, "You better start praying that's a tumour girl!" With that she walked away, picked up the phone, and called a gynecologist/obstetrician I had been seeing for some problems with my menstrual cycle. *He'll get to the bottom of it,* I thought. And then I heard my mum's words; she was not very happy.

"I am bringing my seventeen-year-old daughter in to see the doctor right now. Yes, I

23

realize he is a specialist that requires appointments. He needs to understand that he has been seeing my daughter about her menstruation issues for some time now, and that I just felt her belly and I would say there is about a five-month fetus in there! We will be there shortly."

We drove up to the doctor's office, and I could swear I heard the music from that scene in *The Wizard of Oz* where Almira Gulch peddled away from Dorothy and the farm with Toto in her basket. Dr. Baldwin did his exams, then sent me for an ultrasound and to our family doctor for follow up.

Dr. Olson was a wonderful man and was always so very kind to me. I went in to see him, very young and very pregnant, and said, "I'm not really sure how this happened." His only response was to slowly raise from his stool and move to stare out of the window. I finally asked him what he was doing, and he turned to me and said with a smile, "Well, if you didn't do anything that would cause this to happen, then last time this occurred, three wise men came from the east, and I don't want to miss it." We both laughed. He always knew how to bring humour in at just the right time to put me at ease.

Now, if you are also the child of an old-school RN, you might have a story or two that we could reminisce over. One of mine is my mum and I going for a picnic at White Rock Beach not long after we found out I was pregnant. We laid on a blanket eating some absolutely perfect egg salad sandwiches with the crusts cut off and going over every possible problem that could occur during pregnancy and labour. Mum was an amazing woman who had survived so much trauma, and she was not going to let her daughter be caught off guard by all that could go wrong in life. She taught me from a very young age about things like putting on a good face in public and being prepared to be alone because men leave. In this instance, she told me about prolapsed pelvises, birth defects, and my personal favourite, stillbirth. She never taught me these things out of anger or some kind of horrible cruel streak; she adored me, and she knew what it felt like to be blindsided and abandoned. In her big, beautiful heart, she believed she was protecting me.

As for my little girl mind and imagination, well, she had other ideas.

Mum also informed me during that picnic that I would be marrying Randy, my high school sweetheart and the father of my child, just four days later. She had already set everything up for us, we just needed to show up. And so we did—two teens, an unborn child, and a well-meaning Mum. I'm sure you'll be *shocked* to know that this relationship didn't work out after such a great start.

Being a pregnant teenager can be difficult at any time, but being one in the seventies had its own share of challenges. This was back in the day (oh, how I have always wanted to say that) when it was quite acceptable for people to treat you any way they wanted to, and a pregnant teen was especially low in the pecking order. I had to be in the hospital on bed rest for some time before my daughter Jessica was born—I had gone passed my due date, and there had been some potentially problematic blood work results that they wanted to investigate further. One night, I woke to discover that my bed was wet. I called in this big old nurse, who was very mad that I had woken her up, and informed her that I thought my water had broken. She scowled and said, "You probably peed the bed, you're still a baby yourself." As it turned out, she was wrong. My water had indeed broken, and I would have a baby in the next twenty-four hours.

By the next morning, labour had started moving along slowly. Being quite pregnant, I really had to pee. I asked repeatedly if someone could bring me a bed pan or help me get to the bathroom as I wasn't allowed to get up, but it was so busy that day that the nurses were run off their feet and didn't have time to assist me. Today I would have sorted the situation out by myself, but back then I did what I was told. Trauma had created a way of being that was full of hiding and never really being honest with myself or others. I was afraid of being a problem, of asking for too much, of causing a scene. I was afraid people would be angry with me, that they would get tired of me, that they didn't have time for me. I did not value myself, so why would they? The impact of trauma had left me feeling worthless and unlovable, and asking a perfect stranger for help, even a nurse, seemed to be too much to ask, especially for someone unlovable like me.

The nurses told me that someone would help me when I got down to labour and delivery, but once I arrived, I discovered they were so inundated that people were delivering their babies in the hallway. Once again, I was told to hold it. Then they decided they were doing a caesarean section, and since they were going to put a catheter in, you guessed it, I was told I could wait. I had now been waiting to go to the washroom for over two hours while also in labour, yet I was too afraid to complain.

What happened next would have been humiliating if it wasn't so hilarious. A nice nurse came in and attempted to put the catheter in. I know now that they need to use a child's catheter on me, but they didn't know that on this particular day, so she was struggling. An older nurse came in to help, mad at the other nurse for not getting it done and mad at me for being a burden on society. She grabbed the catheter out of the other nurse's hand and crammed it into my urethra with such force that it pulled the other end right out of the catheter bag. I almost wish I had a video of what happened next; nowadays it probably would have gone viral.

With no bag to stop it, my full bladder began emptying out of that catheter at the rate of a fully cranked garden hose. There I lay, legs spread, apologizing as urine sprayed all over this rather stern nurse. The other nurse was laughing so hard she was doubled over while the older nurse yelled at her to make it stop. It was poetic justice at its best.

My incredible daughter Jess was born that day, and I found myself entering a new stage of life: motherhood. Those early days were a mix of joy and terror. I lived in fear that there was something so wrong with me, and that I would somehow pass that down to her. What if I hurt my little girl? What if I touched her like people had touched me? I had no desire to do such a thing, but that did not stop my fear. This pain and terror reached so far that I was afraid to breastfeed her. My stepmom Sandy, who was very knowledgeable on natural ways of being, did her best to help me, explaining to me how good it would be for Jess and how it would be a beautiful bonding experience for both of us. I tried, I really tried, but unfortunately my understanding of intimacy and physical touch had been confined to unwanted sexual advances for so much of my life that even though breastfeeding never "felt" sexual, I was afraid I was somehow sexually abusing her. I never mentioned this to anyone, though, because I was young and wounded and couldn't find a way to speak those words to anyone. I didn't even recognize that my fears were a result of the abuse I had experienced. I am weeping as I type these words, seeing how much trauma took from me. The long reach of trauma doesn't have to make logical sense; it is insidious and permeates every aspect of our being.

Looking back, I can see that Randy and I really did the best we could and had many happy moments together. We were still teenagers, but we had bought a house and were living a life very much like other couples did in those days. Randy had become a journeyman transmission mechanic while I stayed home with Jessie. We likely both had our share of unresolved issues, but I loved so much about our life together, especially watching Jess grow. The sound of her laughter filled my heart; I can still hear it today. Everything she did seemed amazing to me, and yet there was so much unhealed in me that it was difficult for me to ever fully grasp the love that I felt, even as I was living it.

3

Cryin' Ryan and Learning to Pray

"There are only two ways to live your life. One is as though nothing is a miracle.
The other is as though everything is a miracle."
Albert Einstein

In early 1979, I became pregnant with our second child. This time, I was really excited—I wasn't so young, and I wasn't taken by surprise. This pregnancy started off easier than my first, although I did have some complications later on and was once again kept in the hospital for a few weeks before the birth.

On December 5, a few weeks past my due date, a nurse's voice came over the intercom and asked, "Have you had anything to eat or drink in the last few hours?"

I hurriedly gulped down the chocolate in my mouth and asked, "Why?" I didn't receive an answer. As a pregnant teen, questions were not encouraged; really, they were rather frowned upon.

A few moments later, someone came in and put a "nothing by mouth" sticker on the foot of my bed. I again asked why; this time, the nurse answered. "To get ready for your c-section." This was news to me. I took my quarters down to the phone booth and called my mum and

Randy so that they could come to the hospital to be with me.

I requested—well, begged fearfully—not to be sedated. With my first caesarean, I was given general anesthetic as that was the way things were done back then. In the time between my two deliveries, they had begun doing c-sections with the mother awake and numbed from the chest down. I was a person with many fears as a result of my trauma, and some of my strongest fears were around my body and feeling any lack of control. Thankfully, they agreed.

This was in the early days of people being able to stay awake for a c-section, so they asked if it would be okay for some students to observe. I agreed. I have a vague memory of being in an operating room full of medical students. I was both excited and nervous as the surgery started—laying on a table unable to move with an incision in my abdomen was a rather overwhelming experience. I fondly remember a very kind nurse who stayed with me beyond the end of her shift to help me to stay calm.

Before beginning the surgery, the doctor had asked what names I had chosen. I didn't know whether I was having a boy or a girl—at the time, people typically didn't know this prior to the birth of their child—so I told him both options. My son was born and immediately gave out a loud bellow; the doctor said, "Well, here he is, Cryin' Ryan!"

The celebration was short-lived. The joy turned into looks of concern, and the nurses quickly whisked him away. I was told not to worry, that they just needed to investigate a few things that didn't look quite right. The doctor closed my incision, and I was taken to the recovery room without holding Ryan or understanding exactly what was happening.

That morning, I turned on the news and saw Russia preparing to invade Afghanistan. As I lay in my hospital bed, I thought, *What have I done? What kind of a world have I brought my sweet boy into?*

Unfortunately, troubles were about to hit much closer to home. Ryan was born with some very serious medical conditions—they told us there were antibodies in my blood similar to the RH factor that were destroying his blood. During the first week of his life, Ryan had three complete blood exchanges. This wee little baby would be put onto a table surrounded by all these machines, one line taking the blood out of him and another replacing it. He was so jaundiced that he had passed the yellow point and instead turned green; the nurses affectionately nicknamed him the Incredible Hulk. His spleen was distended and his liver was enlarged. He was not doing well.

On December 20, Randy and I had a meeting with Dr. Ou Tim, who was the attending pediatric specialist. He let us know that he was trying everything he could, but nothing was working. What was happening was very rare—in fact, he had only seen it once before, and that child did not make it. He had the very difficult task of letting us know that the chances of our son surviving were very slim.

Randy and I didn't know how to process this. We were young, so young, so we didn't have the skills to discuss this as a couple. Although really, how does anyone process this news at any age?

That night, my thoughts drifted to a friend who had miscarried earlier that week and something stirred within my heart. I can't really explain why or how this came to me, but I knelt beside my bed and put my hands together in prayer. If you imagine a postcard of a child kneeling beside their bed and clasping their hands together, that was exactly what I looked like. I wasn't raised in a particularly religious family, so I didn't really know how to pray. I just had this feeling that I needed to do something. I said, "Thank you, thank you so much that I got to hold him. My friend never even got to meet her baby. I just wanted to say thank you that I got to hold him and feed him." I didn't really know what else to do, so I said "amen" and went to bed.

The next morning, I got up and phoned the hospital to check on Ryan. I always called into the Intensive Care Nursery before I went in the morning; if I was going to get really bad news, I didn't want to get it in the hospital. I wanted to be somewhere I was comfortable in and familiar with.

When I told the nurse who I was, she responded, "I don't even know what to say to you. I don't know what to tell you." My whole body just froze; I was sure he was dead. As I almost started to cry, she continued, "No, no, no, I'm sorry. I'm sorry. I just mean, he's completely better. He's healed, completely healed. There's nothing wrong with him. We don't understand what happened. He's completely better. His colour is normal. His tummy has gone down. All his blood counts are fine. Everything is fine. It's like there was never anything wrong with him." I told her I had prayed last night, and she said to me, "Well, we've seen a lot of things like that go on around here, so maybe that's what happened. You hold on to that."

Ryan was healthy enough to go home, but since his recovery was so unexpected, they wanted to keep him a few more days to make sure everything continued to go well. Thankfully it did, and I was able to bring Ryan home on Christmas eve. It was amazing, and I was incredibly grateful. To this day, I am still so, so grateful.

Ode to Daniel by Alison Perry-Davies

*For my godson Daniel…like a shooting star; bright, bold,
beautiful and gone too soon.*

*Finding a place of gratitude and
listening to that still, small voice has carried me
through many dark times.*

From that moment on, Ryan just soared through life. He sat up fast, he crawled fast, he walked fast, he talked fast. He excelled at anything he put his mind to.

We had a check up with Dr. Ou Tim when Ryan was a year old. As we walked toward his office, Ryan went running ahead of me. The doctor didn't even have time to get up from his desk—Ryan ran right up, crawled onto his lap, and said "Hi." The doctor's eyes teared up a bit, and he looked at me and said, "I need you to know that this was a miracle. I didn't do this, only God did this. I had done everything that I could do, and there was nothing left. Nothing was working. This is what a miracle looks like."

Finding a place of gratitude and listening to that still, small voice has carried me through many dark times. I continued to search for some understanding of life and the possible meanings behind all we are experiencing, both together and as individuals. Throughout my life, I was always looking for and attracted to spiritual things. Sometimes that was church, sometimes it was psychic fairs and tarot cards, sometimes it was new age ideas. Most often, I simply felt a close connection to spirit/creator/God. I felt drawn to an invisible wave of love that sometimes showed up in visible ways. Just like the miracle that saved my son, gentle whispers would come to me in difficult times and guide me toward what needed to be done.

When my children were two and four years old, Randy and I separated and then divorced. Although there was a lot of unhealthiness in our relationship, neither of us knew much about communication or how to really be in a loving marriage. We were kids having kids, unable to really understand what we needed to do to fix anything that wasn't working in our relationship. Personally, I was a bit of a wild child with a "don't tell me what to do" attitude—I could be a lot of fun, and also rather out of control at times. I was short on life experience and large on unhealed trauma. Oh boy, doesn't that sound fun! What could *possibly* go wrong?

The way I left Randy was the beginning of a pattern of running away, and I am guessing it hurt him deeply. I'm sorry for that. That's not to say that either of us were great at relationships, but as I think of the choices I made in relationships and how I saw life in general, I can now see that I was someone who left, always. I would leave relationships, jobs, and homes; that is how my trauma played out in my life. I had known the pain of abandonment, and through counselling I eventually learned that I had made a vow as a little girl that no one would ever leave me again. So, I left people before they could leave me. Until I found healing, the only people I didn't leave were my kids—and as I look back now, I realize that emotionally, I left them at times too.

My kids and I grew up together. We got into all kinds of shenanigans like swimming in fountains with no trespassing signs, taking off school on occasion just so we could hang out together, and watching movies too late on a school/work night, things that a more mature parent might not choose to do with their children. Kids at school would ask whether I was their big sister, and teachers didn't always take me seriously—at least, that's how I perceived it. The defensiveness of unhealed trauma can distort so much.

We had lots of fun days as well as days where I was a tad out of control. I screamed more than I should have and made a lot of mistakes along the way. There were lots of relationships I was in that my kids didn't get a vote on, lots of moving, lots of new schools. Thankfully, there were also a few relationships—good ones—that I never left. There was my friend Lisa, who was also a single parent to her son (my godson) Daniel. We navigated parenthood and relationships and searching spirituality together. She and Daniel were people we could always count on even as their family grew, with Jen and Andrew and Sheldon joining them over the years. There was also Blondie; my friend Colleen and her sons, Little Johnny and Little Mike; and Dee and her three boys, Mike, Curtis, and Ryan. These friendships mattered not only to me but also to my children. Throughout all the chaos and moves and changes, Jessie and Ryan still knew and visited these people, and having that consistency in their lives was huge for them.

Although there were some really great adventures that came from this life of constantly moving and changing, living under the weight of unhealed trauma created a scenario where I was focused on trying to stop my own pain rather than comprehending that I could and would inevitably cause my children pain. There was never a day I did not adore my children to the very depth of my being; however, consistently finding healthy ways to show that rather than feeling like I needed to somehow protect myself is a lesson I learned a little later than I would have liked.

If I could call on Dr. Who and get him to bring me on a ride in the Tardis, the only thing I would ever change in my life—well, other than buying stocks in Apple or something like that—would be to treat my kids then the way I treat my grandkids now. I would listen more and ask for their opinions on my grand schemes. I would make sure they knew how important they are to me when they were little, and I would make a conscious effort to create a safe space for them rather than indulging whatever idea popped into my mind. I know I could have done better by my kids, yet I still cherish so many parts of our journey together. Through it all, we loved lots and we laughed lots, and I did the best I could with what I had.

4

The Pain That Changed Me

*"If you've been up all night and cried till you have no more tears left in you
—you will know that there comes in the end a sort of quietness."*
C. S. Lewis, *The Lion, the Witch and the Wardrobe*

Even after my kids arrived, I was running, always running, without recognizing the absolute wake I left behind me everywhere I went. By now, I had been raped multiple times, beaten to unconsciousness in an assault and had a string of unhealthy and abusive relationships. I was self-medicating and blaming and finger-pointing and doing anything and everything I could think of to escape from something inside me that was so dark I didn't even know it was there. There were drugs and alcohol and gambling and serial monogamy and religion and shopping and exercise and education and throwing myself into my work and putting myself in dangerous situations. I never saw what I was doing, until I did.

The day I began to change was the day I found out that my sweet girl, my little Jessie doodle, had been sexually assaulted by the husband of the woman who ran the licensed in-home daycare my children attended. A place I had personally checked out. A place I had taken her and Ryan to, ignoring her cries as I dropped her off because I was late for work. I did that, and the road to forgiving myself for this has been much longer than any other I have taken.

There was much that happened before I would reach out for healing; I wasn't through hating myself yet. I wasn't through being angry and lost and full of shame. What I was, though, was desperate. Going through court, taking Jessie for surgery to be repaired from her rape, watching how my son was being impacted, and trying to process it all was more than I was ready to handle at twenty-two years old. I tried anything and everything to find relief from this relentless torment. I even prayed to God and asked him to exact revenge and justice on the person who had done this horrible thing. I didn't want him dead; I wanted him to suffer like he made my daughter suffer. I wanted him to know pain and fear, terrifying fear. If ever there was a time where fire should be falling from heaven, this should be it, right?

One night, after a day of court, I was filled with rage and desperation. Questions and shame haunted me. I started wailing—not crying, wailing a guttural torment from so deep within me that I could not bear the weight of it. I needed to know how God could let this happen. *Did you watch and get off on it? Is that what you were doing? You sick bastard! What kind of a god are you? I hate you! You could have stopped it! You could have saved her! You could have saved her body and her mind and all of her, and you just watched!*

I screamed until my throat was raw. I screamed until I vomited. I screamed until the muscles in my body could not bear the intensity and I dropped to the floor like a ragdoll. It was the most honest I have ever been with anyone in my entire life, and at the end of it, I had nothing left.

I lay there whimpering on the floor for hours. There was no place of comfort; no all-knowing, all-loving God to call on. He had his chance, and this was what happened.

I was alone.

After that night, I spent a long time feeling lost. The one good that came from it, if there is such a thing, is that I learned I needed to make some changes. I needed to find a way—some way, any way—to give my kids a life that would be safe. One tiny step at a time, I began a journey to find a way to offer hope and stability to my children, even though I wasn't necessarily sure this was an achievable goal—I was still pretty messed up. If I am being really honest with myself, I didn't think I had much hope for my own life getting better; I just knew I needed to at least give my children a chance.

As the court case continued, there came a day when it became clear to me I needed to help my kids have a life that was more than whatever I was doing with them. Counselling was offered to us, and truthfully, I only said yes for Jess and Ryan. I didn't really see the need for me to go—after all, I wasn't the one going around raping kids. Thus began the very first steps down my path to healing.

The following years were filled with many ups and downs as I tried to make sense of what happened. I studied the brain, science, spirituality, and religion. I drank wine beyond what was healthy. I ate more than I should have, stuffing my feelings with every mouthful. I hated and judged and made choices that were harmful to myself and those around me. I laughed, I cried, I felt terror and pain. Sometimes I was paralyzed with fear, other times I took risks that made no sense. All the while I was writing poetry as a way to process and release all that I was feeling.

I also started to sing in bands and danced across the stages as I did, and yet I somehow still hid from the world, always finding ways to disguise my truest self. I craved attention, and yet I was afraid to be noticed. My life was an out of control carousel that had come off the tracks—a train wreck desperately looking for ways to quiet the shame.

In an effort to find someone who could give me all the answers I was seeking, I reached out to mystics and healers. I also tried several churches and was told that I needed to forgive the man who had abused my daughter—I wasn't even speaking about my own abuse yet, except for in counselling sessions. It was hard for me to accept that a god or a belief system might require or even suggest that I needed to consider forgiveness, not after what this man had done.

A deep healing began about twenty years after that night when I wept and accused God of so many things. Since I was a child, I have had dreams, visions, feelings, and intuitions that feel more like they came from a collective energy outside of myself, rather than from my own imagination. This was one such occurrence. In this dream, I saw the man who had raped my daughter being brought before a judgement throne of sorts. In that place, there was nowhere to hide—not from judgement and not from himself. Any of the stories he could have told himself to justify his actions against my daughter and other children were completely stripped away. And then there came over him an absolute understanding of what he had done. It was not simply knowing the deeds, but rather an undeniable understanding of the suffering he had caused.

His agony was like nothing I had ever seen before; it was as if he was burning from the inside out. It was absolutely excruciating to witness. Here was a person who had done unthinkable things to my daughter and caused so much pain, and yet I was almost feeling compassion for him in his torment.

In that moment, I was reminded of the times I had done things which were so much smaller than his abuses and yet still haunt me. And it was then that I saw we all have a choice: we can face what we have done here and now and do whatever it takes to come to the fullest possible understanding of the hurt we have caused, or we can wait and it will be shown to us.

I awakened sobbing. The intensity of this dream was such that I actually had compassion in my heart for this man who had done so much damage. My hate and my anger toward him were beyond what I can describe, and yet there I was feeling compassion for him. There were places in me that felt angry about that too.

I wish I had words that could adequately capture the weight I felt as I carried that dream around with me for days and weeks and months. This vision was part of a very long and lonely path I had been travelling towards forgiveness. There were many twists and turns along the way, all part of guiding me towards healing.

We all have our time in the wilderness, I suppose—a time where we feel lost and alone and have no way of knowing how to get back, or even where we might go back to. I am guessing that most people who come from layers of trauma have had such experiences. Some, myself included, have had several.

Another of these times came much later in my life, after I became a nana. Many people had recommended I read a book called *The Shack* by William P. Young. I didn't know much about it, but I decided to go ahead and read it. I was completely unprepared for the content of the book or the dark places it would take me.

This simple book was the hardest 256 pages I have ever read. It is about the healing journey of a father whose daughter, Missy, is kidnapped and does not survive. I am not ruining the book for you by telling you this—it happens in the very beginning, and there is nothing graphic shared about the incident. Yet a child being taken leaves much to the imagination about the horrors that wee one faced.

When I reached the part where Missy first went missing, my body started to respond quite intensely to the mere thought of such a situation. An anger rose in me that I had not felt for a very long time—an anger towards God.

I wept for many hours that night and into the morning. As the light started to peer through my drapes, I told God through my tears, "It stops here! If you let anything happen to Hannah [my granddaughter], that will be it. I will never forgive you!!" My guts were wrenched, my teeth were clenched, and I was spitting as I spoke those words.

With everything that was in me, I believed three things that night. First, I believed that there was, indeed, a God. Second, I believed that he had somehow allowed my mum, myself, and my sweet daughter to be abused. Third, I believed that if it happened to my granddaughter Hannah as well, if he allowed that, then I would hate him all the days of my life, and I would happily go to hell and hate him there too.

Once again, I found myself being more honest in that moment than I had ever been, either with myself or with my God. I was so far past being a mindless follower who would never question God; I was a mum and a nana and a survivor.

There have been many studies that have shown how trauma and trauma-related stress is passed down from one generation to another. There is even evidence that our environment affects gene expression and cellular activity, suggesting that our traumas may be passed down through our very DNA if they are not addressed. I am not going to try to understand, and certainly not going to try to explain, what many people with multiple degrees and decades of experience are still working to comprehend. What I will say is that there appears to be evidence that we are impacted by generational trauma in one way or another—recurring, ongoing, hereditary trauma that is relived over and over again.

I saw this in happen in my own life. My mum was abused, and then I was abused, and then my daughter was abused. It took me years to even see my own trauma and recognize the impact it had had on my life, but once I saw it, I was unstoppable. I needed to be able to be free of it so that I could help my daughter and son find a way out and protect my grandkids from ever knowing this pain.

It is one thing to realize that there is generational trauma or curses in our life, but breaking the cycle is another. If there are chains binding me and my family to this trauma, then how do we break free? How do we live whole, healthy lives? I needed to find a way to generational healing and a way to see the beautiful generational blessings that were right in front of me come into fruition.

To achieve this, I knew I had to figure out what that path forward would look like. I know from experience, both personal and professional, how easy it is to be stuck in what I have called the "rearview mirror focus" rather than the "windshield focus." I came up with this analogy when I was working as a disability case manager and would use this with my

Washed Away by Alison Perry-Davies

The feeling of globs of paint on my brush as it glides across the canvas is so soothing to me. It brings peace and comfort as well as a connection and grounding that allows everything else to fall away as I put my focus forward, living in the moment and embracing the healing that comes with it.

clients and in my own life. Basically, whether we are driving our cars or living our life, it is our focus that directs us—where we put our focus is where we travel to. It is one thing to check our rearview mirror periodically when we drive—to look back on what has happened so that we may learn from it and ensure there is nothing coming from behind us that could harm us. However, it would be dangerous to try to move forward while keeping our gaze fixed on the past or the rearview mirror. I have found this to be a wonderful way to remind myself and my clients to be mindful of which direction we are focussing on.

It took me almost four years to get through *The Shack*, and when I finally finished, I painted one of my favourite paintings I have ever created. It is an abstract piece that helped me completely release all my feelings around a particularly impactful scene from the book. If you intend to read *The Shack*, I recommend skipping this next paragraph.

In one part of the book, Mack is able to see Missy through a waterfall. He can see that she is in heaven, and that she is alive, healthy, and happy. This powerful experience helps Mack to find peace as he now believes that she is okay and that she is safe. As I read those pages, I felt a connection to the knowing that even with enormous suffering and grief, there can be beauty on the other side. The waterfall felt soothing and healing, and I wanted to find a way to express all that was inside of me. I knew I needed to paint, and that I needed to do it without thinking about how the painting would turn out or if it would look like a waterfall. None of that mattered to me; what mattered was the feeling of the paint: steady and flowing, serene.

The feeling of globs of paint on my brush as it glides across the canvas is so soothing to me. It brings peace and comfort as well as a connection and grounding that allows everything else to fall away as I put my focus forward, living in the moment and embracing the healing that comes with it.

When the Darkness Comes

BY ALISON PERRY-DAVIES

When the darkness comes
It hovers like a cloud for days
I can feel it
Taunting me
Reminding me
Threatening me

It feels heavy
And cyclical
Like it needs to run its course
Only then will it leave me alone for a while

When the darkness hovers
I stay still
Reminding myself it isn't really happening now
It is just a bully that mocks me

The darkness and wine
Are seldom good friends
And never to be entertained
Simultaneously

When the darkness comes
Things feel extreme
They feel urgent
The threat feels closer than my breath

When the darkness comes
It is as if there is no skin on my body
My nerve endings are raw
Exposed

Everything feels more
More Intense
More Severe
Overwhelming

When the darkness comes
I am cautious
It is best to avoid people and places and things
Stay hidden and quiet and safe

Eat healthy
Lay low
Run from sugar and certain shows and sounds
And anything and everything that feeds this beast

When the darkness comes it lies
It tells me it will never leave
It can be so difficult to remember
Times of freedom and of peace

When the darkness comes
I take cover
I remind myself how far I have come
I find my way back to the light

When the darkness comes

5

Mentors and Other Marvels

"If I have seen further, it is by standing on the shoulders of giants."
Sir Isaac Newton

Long before I began working on recovering from my trauma, my mum was already laying the foundation for my healing journey. She spent the last seventeen years of her nursing career working in a mental health facility called Riverview Hospital. Perhaps because she had known emotional pain so intimately, she carried with her a huge, compassionate heart and a desire to bring peace to those who suffered.

From the time I was about twelve years old, Mum would bring us kids with her to the dances at Penn Hall, which was located on the grounds of the hospital. It was important to Mum that we were around people who might look and act differently than us, and that we found a way to be okay with that. She was teaching us inclusion decades before anyone spoke of such things.

When there were female residents who were ready to be released and didn't have family members willing to bring them home, my mum would invite them to spend their weekends with us. She told us, "Right now they only see themselves as mentally ill, and that is all they will ever be if we don't remind them of who they are." I don't recall having strong feelings about any of this at the time, but as an adult, I was profoundly impacted by the realization of all that Mum had taught me and my brothers. And with each new phase of my life—becoming a parent, finding my way to healing, serving others—I have come to a deeper understanding and appreciation of everything our incredible mother had been teaching us.

As life went on and I experienced abuses and losses and wonderful moments—all of what my life would be—I naturally felt drawn to healing, creating, and spiritual ways of being. I could no more choose not to be that way than I could choose not to breathe; it seems to be a requirement for my survival. More and more, I could see that for all the difficulties I have faced, I have also been blessed in so many ways. From a very young age, I have been mentored, taught, and had rich experiences poured into my life. I didn't always recognize what I was being given at the time, but today I am very grateful for the people who took the time to teach me, even when I was quite unteachable.

One person who had a huge influence on my life was a wonderful woman named Maggie Collins whom I met when I was in my early twenties. Maggie was the mother of a friend of mine and worked as a career counsellor. She had a wonderful Irish accent, a huge heart, and a no-nonsense way about her. Maggie had been a single mom to five children for many years while her husband was in prison, an experience that could have been challenging for just about anyone. Not Maggie, though. She found a way to soar, and she was so dedicated to seeing others find their own way.

When I met Maggie, she saw something in me and encouraged me to explore, learn, and find my way in life. She helped me see that I could create whatever life I wanted and help others along the way. Once again, the value of serving others and practicing gratitude was being instilled in me. She also told me that no matter what level of education I ended up with—I had planned to study social work but put that on hold when I became pregnant with Jessie—I should never stop volunteering and never stop learning. I took those words to heart, and I have never regretted a moment of it.

My first volunteer position was in about 1980 at Lifeline, a crisis and suicide intervention phone line based out of Coquitlam, BC. I was required to take an eight-week course that covered active listening skills, crisis and suicide intervention and prevention, what community resources were available, and how we could assist our clients to access them.

46

This was the beginning of my love for studying psychology, sociology, counselling, healing, communication, and all the ways we can connect with each other.

In the mid-eighties, once things started to settle after Jess's assault, I started exploring what it might take to work with other families who had been through similar situations. I began studying social sciences at first, then psychology and sociology for three years. Learning about what could go right and wrong in a person's psyche was fascinating to me. I went on to study different counselling modalities, earning certificates and diplomas along the way. I studied the humanistic approach to counselling as well as several Christian and spiritual-based approaches, and in all of them I found overlaps and connections between the science of the brain as well as more emotional and spiritual aspects. I also studied nutrition and the impacts of what we put into our bodies on every level of our being—mind, body, spirit, and emotion. I was studying holistic wellness long before I recognized it as such. I was drawn to the layers and intricacies of us as beings and how we connect with others, with ourselves, and with the invisible realm, whether that be intuition or God or spirit. It became more and more clear to me that in some ways these aspects are unique, and in other ways they are always working together.

Throughout this time, I was also playing with a few bands in different clubs throughout the area. To me, music is a person, a place, and a thing—a pathway and a destination and a companion. Whether I am playing music or listening to it, music is and has always been my safe place. As a child, I would stand in front of my mirror and sing with a brush as my microphone. Music would take me to a place that was both deep inside of me and somehow completely outside of myself all at once. It soothed me and excited me and helped me to explore feelings I was often too afraid to look at. Music was my healer and my surgeon and my friend. As an adult, singing with a band and letting everything out left me feeling powerful and vulnerable all at once.

During my time as a worship leader in churches, I experienced music at an even deeper level of intimacy, finding ways to connect to creation and the creator. In a spirit-led worship service, it is not so much about songs with beginnings and endings as one might be used to experiencing elsewhere. For example, for many years my husband and I were part of a church community where we would worship through music, dance, painting, and other art forms. As we were singing, we would linger on one song for a very long time if it felt like there was a breakthrough coming. People used the music and the moment and the spirit itself as a conduit to release what was not serving them and embrace what would. I was actively experiencing and participating in holistic healing through creativity long before I had the language to describe it.

I have spent time singing in bars, clubs, restaurants, and churches, sometimes with bands and even doing karaoke. In the early nineties, karaoke became popular and expanded out from Chinatown into the mainstream pubs. When this happened, my brother Doug, my sister-in-law Jody, and I bought some equipment and started a business that ran karaoke events. At first I did all the shows, but over time we purchased a few machines and hired staff so that we could operate in multiple locations each night.

Through connections I had made over the years, I was invited to go into some institutions and retirement homes to do karaoke during the day. In each of these places, the residents' faces would light up when I came in, and I would encourage them to sing along with me. I didn't recognize or label what I was doing as a form of music therapy; I just knew that music has a way of finding its way into our hearts when nothing else could and making space so we could feel whole again. Soon word spread and I started being invited to other hospitals, group homes, care homes, and day programs to offer "music therapy." I wasn't sure what to call what I was doing; I just knew that I loved to see these people smile. Later, when I was studying for my diploma in Holistic Creative Therapy, I learned even more about using music and art in a therapeutic way. It was wonderful to discover that I had been using so many of these methods long before I had a name for them.

I have always been very interested in spiritual concepts and felt a longing for and drawing to spirit. For many years, I explored and studied many of the mystics as well as some new age philosophies. Then, in the mid-nineties, I decided to go to Bible college and study ministry and theology. Through this, I learned so much not just about the Bible but also, and more importantly, about love. The classes were taught by people from a variety of denominations, some with contrary beliefs and views—this opened my mind and heart and encouraged me to learn even more. Once again, I had a person much like Maggie who mentored me for many years. Dr. Tom Saunders was a history professor, a musician, a pastor, and a friend. He taught me about serving and loving and accepting people where they are at rather than where we want them to be. Looking back, it is so clear to me that he was living that example loud and clear through treating me as the person he saw I could and would be rather than the person I was at the time. True love—love that sees us and accepts us where we are at—is something

I wish for every person to have in their life. It takes no great gifting to point out flaws. I have known that love, and now I do my best to share it with the world.

Tom pastored our church alongside Dave Hixson, and both demonstrated an incredible level of compassion. They showed me that true "prophetic ministry" sees all we are capable of and fans that flame through acceptance and kindness.

Everywhere I went, I saw that music and all forms of creativity were bringing freedom, hope, and healing to so many people. After graduating from Bible college, I went on to work in ministry and counselling, supporting people with a variety of mental health and cognitive challenges. I was still a worship leader, leading people in song and finding spaces to connect to spirit, as well as playing in bars with friends and with different bands. I also spent many years working at group homes and day programs for adults living with a variety of cognitive challenges. My coworkers were predominantly artists, creatives, and musicians, and we would make use of that during our down time with our clients. There would be singing and dancing and painting and love and laughter. People were finding ways to explore and express all that was inside of them, and I was honoured to be a small part of that process.

Sometimes I was invited to go into group homes and day programs as a "storyteller." I would read a book out loud or sometimes make up stories on the spot, and it was so wonderful to see how people would be taken out of where they were and what they were experiencing, even for an hour. This was another beautiful opportunity to share in small, simple steps toward loving others and bringing them life and joy.

Looking back now, it is clear to me that I have been living my life as a holistic practitioner for decades. I believe that it has much to do with living out our calling or destiny—it is something that unfolds and blossoms as we explore what catches our interest. I know some people cringe at the word holistic, and I get it—it is a word that is overused and misused, creating the sense that it is a generic phrase much like "natural" that you can slap on a product to help it sell. For me, though, "whole-istic" is about seeing a person and a situation in its entirety. Looking at my life and my healing from a holistic and integrative perspective means to *me* that I want to be sure to look at every aspect: mind, spirit, body, and emotion.

In the early 2000s, right around the time of my PTSD diagnosis, I started to explore some more ways of healing, growing, and seeing the world. I was in a leadership position at the time, so I was invited to attend a powerful week-long course facilitated by a man named Jim McNeish. He had some teachings on the "deeper magic" from *The Lion, the Witch, and the Wardrobe*, and I was so impacted by his teachings that I later named one of my businesses Deeper Magic. The magic, of course, is love. In his two-part workshop, McNeish took us on a journey of self-discovery and showed us ways to be with ourselves and with others. He had a wonderful way of communicating, and he taught others to communicate at a much more honest and honouring level. As the workshop progressed, I really started to see that I was about to be part of something so powerful—I just had to find the courage to take a step out into a place not yet discovered. I was given another layer of finding ways to understand and accept myself or to change whatever I found lacking.

Throughout the workshops, I was given glimpses into all that could and would be in my life. While we were doing a type of visualization exercise, I had such a clear vision of myself standing in complete darkness. In this vision, love was standing with me, inviting me to take a step off of a cliff. I was so frightened, and yet I somehow knew that I would be okay. Each time I took a step into the darkness, my foot would land on a stone which would then become illuminated to me. I see so much of this vision coming to life now, and it is more than I had dared to hope for.

In 2008, I went to an amazing conference for the arts called "Shatter" in Dallas, Texas, put on by Keith and Sanna Luker. I was now eight years into healing and understanding the impact of trauma, yet my anxiety was still in control in many ways. In fact, as I arrived at the airport and went to board the plane, I was literally shaking and crying.

My husband David said to me, "My gosh, you don't need to do this. You don't have to go."

I replied, "I do though, I really do need to do this." So, I spoke to my terror and said, *Look, we're doing this no matter what.* And then I got on the plane and went. I learned about physics and music and art and healing and love, and it was a life-changing experience. I didn't rid myself of my anxiety or suddenly heal from the impact of trauma; it was one more layer of healing, one more step towards freedom.

By now Mum was living with Parkinson's and vascular dementia, so she came to live with my husband Dave and me. I stepped down from ministry for a while to care for her, and I spent my time hanging out with her and playing music. With these new living arrangements, I wanted to find work that would allow me to arrange my own schedule. I thought that business would be a good route to achieve this goal, so I took a one-year program through Business Victoria and then started my production business, through which I promoted artists. That was a project of the heart, though, and I soon discovered that I would need more money to make it a success and made the decision to fold the business. However, I had been smitten by the business bug and decided to study it more.

Human resources seemed like a good fit with my counselling background, so I went back to college at fifty and earned an advanced diploma in human resources management. I loved how so much of what I had learned through studying psychology, counselling, and ministry all blended so beautifully with this. And even though I ended up deciding not to pursue a career in HR, these studies helped me find a more linear way to approach much of what I already knew. I am chuckling as I type this because most people likely wouldn't think of HR in that way, but for an artsy type, well, it was pretty linear.

I wanted to use my skill set in a way that would be both helpful and fulfilling, and I found exactly that in the British Columbia Aboriginal Network on Disabilities Society (BCANDS). I worked there as a disability case manager, providing services to Indigenous people living on or off reserve in British Columbia. Neil Belanger is the Executive Director there, and even though he is a curmudgeon and we often argued, he taught me many things. I have no words to express all that I learned in my years working for that organization serving those amazing people. I have Indigenous people in my family, so I think I thought I knew a bit more about this community than your average middle-aged white woman. I had no idea all I would learn—about them, about me, about all of us. I witnessed how systemic racism is alive and well in our country, even today. I met people who changed me in a beautiful way as we learned to trust and understand each other. I was privileged and humbled as I took statements from clients going through the truth and reconciliation process for survivors of the "Indian" residential schools. I heard things that I cannot unhear and they cannot unlive. I saw the beauty of people relearning their culture and the darkness that comes when art and dance and song and spirituality is ripped from them. I also saw the healing power of having these things restored, creativity bringing healing once again.

In 2020, I began a course to become certified in Holistic Integrated Creative Arts Therapy (HICAT). This course has brought together all that I have studied, experienced, and intuitively known throughout my life.

Other important teachers in my life have been dogs—rescues, specifically—as they have been a huge part of my life and my healing. All the dogs I've had over the years have loved music so much. In fact, for any type of creativity I have been involved in, my dogs have always stuck close by me and seemed so comforted by it. There is something about the way a dog, and I think especially a rescue, is able to love at such a deep level. I really like that little poster that says "Please God, make me the person my dog thinks I am"; it speaks volumes about how much they love us. I know many people love cats and other animals, and that is all wonderful too. For me, I'm a dog girl, through and through. To care for another being and have them only have love to give back is a beautiful thing, and I know many people with PTSD, myself included, have benefited from having service dogs as part of our healing process.

While not all of these paths were taken specifically to help with my own healing process, I benefitted from all of these lessons and teachings as much as the people I worked with did. I have found that when we allow ourselves to be teachable and let our intuition be our guide, we are led to exactly where we need to be.

Sammie and Me
Photo by Alison Perry-Davies

6

Brain Trauma and Other Things We Don't Plan For

"There will come a time when you believe everything is finished.
That will be the beginning."
Louis L'Amour

Like many such journeys, my path to healing has had many setbacks. Some days it felt like I was moving backwards just as much as I was moving forward. Yet slowly, things started to improve. Slowly, I learned to recognize my triggers before they happened. Slowly, I started to learn how to best take care of myself. Slowly, I learned to forgive.

Then came 2015, and life changed in a way I never could have seen coming.

Valentine's Day that year started like any other Saturday. The sun was shining particularly bright that morning as I headed out on my scooter to visit Mum. She was living in a complex care facility at the time as she now required twenty-four-hour medical care and a space that supported those needs. I had been visiting her daily, and Dave and I had recently decided we wanted her to come back and live with us. To do that, we needed a larger place that could accommodate her mobility assists and care workers—in fact, we were going to look at a house that afternoon. I was so looking forward to having Mum living with us again so that we could spend more time together and so that she would be with family.

In general, life was going great. Dave and I were doing really well, both as individuals and as a couple. My healing from past trauma had reached a point where I was living a very full life. We were financially comfortable, and we had so much to be grateful for.

After a wonderful visit with my mum, I headed over to the march for missing and murdered Indigenous women in downtown Victoria. There were drums and hugs and friends, and we all gathered and remembered why we were there. I headed home, and then Dave and I put Sammie, our new German shepherd puppy, into her harness in the backseat of the truck and headed out to see what might become our new home. It was so exciting!

And then, in an instant, everything changed.

My lawyer later told me that a young woman had dropped some French fries onto the floor of the backseat while she was driving. She reached around for them, and when she looked up, there we were.

It is surprising how hard a tiny little car can hit a pickup truck. The impact and all that surrounded it is still fuzzy to me. Mostly, what I remember is feeling like something was ripping off the top of my scalp. If you have ever had your eyebrows waxed, you will know the feeling of them putting the wax on your brow, then that piece of paper, and then ripping it off in quick motion. That is how it felt—like someone ripped a strip about three inches wide and six inches long off the top of my head. I vaguely remember talking to a police officer who was trying to get me to go to the hospital, but I just wanted to go home. It was all I could think of.

We did go to a walk-in clinic later that day, and then on Monday I went to my own doctor. What we hoped was a concussion that would settle in a few weeks instead turned out to be a brain injury that has had a long-lasting impact on my life.

The first months and even years after the accident are very much a blur to me. However, I recently read the journal I kept at the time, and it was really hard for me to think back on those days. I was in so much pain; the headaches were overwhelming. I could not be around any lights or sounds, and the vertigo and tinnitus completely took over my life. People would think I had been drinking because I slurred so badly and staggered when I walked. My mind was jumbled, and I literally would forget what I was talking about mid-sentence. The odd part is that much of this wasn't as difficult for me as it was for the people close to me because for the most part, I wasn't aware of my actions. I didn't see that I was irrational or stopping mid-sentence or slurring or staggering. I did know I was crying a lot for reasons I only now understand were part of my brain injury. I could not bear to be around conversations or other noises, so I became a recluse and isolated myself. It was not safe for me to go for walks as I was a fall risk; one fall resulted in a broken toe, another caused my eye to bleed. We had to be careful because any further injury to my brain would be very serious.

It was almost three years before I could drive again as I was considered impaired. I was experiencing severe vertigo and confusion, and I was basically living with no rear view mirror as I could not remember anything behind me for quite some time. I would explain this to people by having them sit in a chair and look forward, then asking them to describe what was behind them. It is an impossible task—as far as your eyes are concerned, there is nothing but blackness back there. That is what it was like (and still is, to some extent). There was a void in my memory; anything back there was just blackness. I wasn't really frightened by that until I became aware of it.

When I first started driving, I had to phone home a few times as I would become lost quite easily if I ventured out further than about a five-kilometre radius. Dave set our GPS up with a home button so I could find my way back if I became a bit lost and panicked. He put the address as being a few blocks from where our home actually was, though, so that no one could find the GPS and know where we lived. Thirty-two years in the military makes for a person who thinks of everything.

Even to this day, I can no longer do the job I loved at BCANDS. I am unable to track client information, maintain conversations, or work for more than an hour or so without becoming confused and having my vertigo and headaches flare up. Even while I was writing this book, I could only work for about an hour before having to stop. If I push myself too hard, the consequences are quite severe—I will likely have to spend the next few days recovering in a darkened room.

Music, once the centre of my life, was taken from me. I could no longer cope with the sensations that music created in my brain. For the first years I could not play, sing, or listen to music without experiencing severe symptoms. I could not even *think* about music without it creating a swirl of dizziness and headaches; the vibration and sounds were more than I could bear.

There are many people and places and things that have been incredibly helpful to me as I learn to live with my "new brain," as I call it. The Victoria Brain Injury Society has been amazing. They are kind and helpful and supportive and offer classes on learning to live with

Glorious Morning by Alison Perry-Davies

I was looking for a way to express what was happening inside of me after my brain injury, so I started to paint. This was my first painting I ever painted and was inspired by a photograph I took on Easter morning.

*Music, once the centre of my life, was taken from me.
I could no longer cope with the
sensations that music created in my brain.*

this new brain, including one I took called Acquired Brain Injury 101. One lesson I took from this class is that people with brain injuries will often over-share, including telling people that we have a brain injury. It is so very, very true. If we are talking while standing close together, I might wonder if I have bad breath and then ask you whether or not I do. Or, I might ask if I am speaking too loud. It's like having a pebble in your shoe; it will likely be all you can think of until you are able to remove it. THAT is life with a brain injury. I am often wondering if I am sharing too much—if people can tell I don't remember what they just said.

One of the challenging parts of living with a brain injury is that I don't want people to talk to me like I am a child or like I am broken, and I don't want them to treat me like I am unable to make a decision on my own. I am doing my best to figure out how to live this new way of being where things can change in a moment. Sometimes, being around people and having to factor in how they might respond to how I am feeling is overwhelming, and there are so many days I would rather just not have to use up what precious energy I have to balance it all. Brain injuries are like that. Trauma is like that. All kinds of grief are like that. All we can do is do what we can, when we can.

Dave and I didn't buy that house we were going to see the day of the accident, and Mum never came home with us. And sadly, my daily visits stopped. I used to visit her for long periods of time; I would bring her breakfast most mornings and we would visit and laugh. After the accident, I couldn't drive for a few years as my vertigo was so intense, and even when I was able to get there, the sounds and lights in the care facility were too much for me to bear for long.

Of all the things I don't remember, somehow I can so clearly picture my sweet mum saying to me, "I miss you so much, I am so lonely." That one haunts me.

The first months of my recovery were the last months of Mum's life. She passed away on October 7, 2015, just under eight months after the accident. I am grateful I was able to be at

57

her bedside for the last few days, and I miss her every day.

This has been another loss, another trauma, another reason to find a way to forgive. That young woman who was picking up her French fries likely has no idea the pain she caused that day—to me, to my mum, and to my family. Her mistake was careless and the cost was huge, but it was just that: a mistake. I do not believe that the impact she had on my life was intentional, and forgiving her was necessary for me to move forward. I wish her well, and I hope she learned from it.

Once again, I needed to learn to live with a significant trauma in my life. I found myself looking for ways to bring healing through creativity, and so I found myself painting. I had never painted before, but there was a knowing somewhere inside of me that I needed to do something creative, and I was unable to write, read, or play music.

The very first image I ever painted was a sunrise from our porch on Easter morning. It was such a beautiful sight that I took a picture of it, and then I thought, *I should paint this.* And so it began.

At first, I could only paint for about two minutes before needing to rest, and then five, and then ten. I was able to pour my feelings into my paintings, and it gave me hope. Creativity, my old friend, found a new way to enter my life and help me through the hard times.

Writing this book has also been an amazing experience. I had started working on it before the accident and then never finished it. I now know my story wasn't ready until now. In the last few years, the opportunity arose to work my way back into writing. I wrote a chapter in one of the Woman of Worth books with Christine Awram, and then another, and then a third collaborative book about mother and son relationships with Rebecca Harrison in her *Family Tree* series. Through these opportunities, I met the amazing talent that is Julie Ann of Influence Publishing, and working with her has been a wonderfully healing experience. She has been incredibly patient and gracious while helping me bring this book into the world; my ability to process words is still somewhat compromised.

Writing and painting have been wonderful ways for me to process and let go of the challenges I am faced with throughout my life, and accepting my "new brain" has certainly been a challenge. Even today, I am still finding new ways to approach my favourite activities so that they don't overwhelm me. I have to take things a little easier these days, but I am still moving forward, always looking for new ways to get back to the things I love.

Part 2

A Path to Healing

7

Trauma's Many Disguises

"The attempt to escape from pain is what creates more pain."
Gabor Maté

Healing from trauma is often as complex as trauma itself. I have found there are no simple fixes but rather a series of steps towards wholeness. When I look back to the beginning of this journey, back to those early days after Jessie's assault when I was first starting along this path, I can see that one of the first steps was recognizing my triggers and how trauma was manifesting in my life.

Trauma and triggers do not come with announcements that say, "Hey, look, it's me, and I am showing up to you in this way right now until you deal with me." Instead, we experience a series of difficult events and feelings, and we make choices based on those experiences. With some time and some help, we learn to recognize that these choices are informed by our trauma. Only then can change take place.

We are not simply victims with no recourse, and in later chapters I will talk about ways to "keep our tank full" and do all we can to be physically, emotionally, and spiritually healthy enough to cope with those triggers. Right now, though, I want to share how trauma showed up in my life and what my triggers could look like. One of the most important lessons I needed to learn was that for me, triggers do not appear as triggers—they come as a real-time, real-life problem, often with no conscious connection to a particular memory or event. It's more of an uneasy feeling that can range from anxiety all the way to feeling overwhelmed with terror.

These feelings are so strong, and yet in the moment we can forget to even question why we are so consumed with reacting. Once we learn to recognize how trauma appears in our life, we are then able to take action to work towards healing it.

There were days when my trauma visited as anxiety and completely dominated my every thought. Even something as simple as going for a walk with a dear friend could be overwhelming. The usually enjoyable conversation would feel more like a blackberry bush entangling me, and I would be left trying to find a way to move that would not leave me twisted and cut. My mind would race, and I would smile and nod and hope they wouldn't notice that absolutely nothing they were saying was getting to a place where I could process it. I would try to hide what was going on inside, still falling back on that belief that I should never tell, ever. This huge secret looming over my life, this darkness, must stay secret.

Yet even in these moments, the sun rested gently across my face and a soft breeze brought with it whispers of hope. I would do my best to just keep walking and smiling, wishing that it would be tomorrow because maybe tomorrow would be better.

There were also days when my trauma manifested as depression, and in some ways that was a welcome reprieve. Where anxiety haunts and taunts, depression has a dark hiddenness to it that lulled me in. I would retreat from the world for days at a time, staying cocooned in a dark room with my heated bean bag held against me, reminding me that there is comfort. I wouldn't answer the phone, and if someone texted, I would politely reply that I was in the middle of something. I wouldn't want to talk or even move. I would feel like if I could just cuddle my dog and lay there, then maybe, just maybe, I would make it to tomorrow.

Some days I would find myself on my second or third bottle of wine, laughing inappropriately and becoming louder and louder, avoiding the darkness by staying in a manic-like party-girl state. Sometimes the self-medication would lubricate the pain just enough to spill it across whatever conversation I was taking over. I would then spend the next few days smothered by shame over words I had spoken while in an alcohol-induced fantasy of being able to say whatever came into my mind because life is wonderful. Dark secrets and several glasses of Chardonnay don't go well together.

Some days I would shop, looking for just the right top or skirt or chair or purse or shoes or skin care to distract me from the horror I was trapped in. I wasn't even looking for a cure, just something that would capture my attention and let me pretend for a while that everything was okay. For the most part, though, I was completely unaware that I was actually using these to distract myself.

Food was another source of distraction. A bag of chips, extra salty, was just enough to let me forget for a moment the voices in my mind that jeered and mocked and threatened me. They were so loud, yet not one person could hear them, nor could they hear my pleading and begging for it to stop. Another sandwich might lessen the volume, just for a moment.

Some days, the reign of terror came over me with an energy that I knew could only be calmed with exercise. This was not intended to create health and wholeness; no, exercise like this is, at its core, restless and troubled. Those days I could spend hours hiking, then go to the gym for a few more hours in a frantic frenzy. The one good thing about reacting to triggers in this way is that exercise releases endorphins, which is one of the ways we can find true healing and improve our ability to cope.

There were days, weeks, even months where I would be paralyzed with fear that I was sick. This was not as simple as being a hypochondriac; it was something much more sinister. I lived in terror that there was something inside my body that was hurting me, and that people either wouldn't believe me if I told them or would be angry with me. Once again, it was a secret I must keep. It does not take a degree in psychology to understand where this fear came from: since I was a little girl, things had been put in my body that hurt me. I once spent two days in pain, too afraid to say anything because I might be imagining it, only to have to rush to the hospital with a ruptured appendix. This sword cuts two ways: it had me afraid that there was something damaging within me, and also that I was imagining it. I have lived for decades with this fear, and to this day I must be diligent about not letting those thoughts in, while also taking care of my body.

One fascinating impact of trauma, which I first noticed in my work as a disability case manager, is what I call the "triple A's": allergies, asthma, and arthritis. Studies have shown that in cases of trauma or chronic stress, our body may respond by triggering an immune response that creates inflammation. Normally, this inflammation is short-lived and serves to protect our body from bacteria, viruses, or pathogens. In the case of trauma or stress, though, this inflammation can become chronic, which is a risk factor for cardiovascular, pulmonary, dermatological, and autoimmune conditions as well as chronic pain. After seeing the three A's over and over in clients living with the impact of trauma, I was then able to recognize them in myself.

When trauma was visiting me, I may have responded or reacted to situations in a way that seems alien or inappropriate to others. Within my perception, though, I was reacting in a way that felt quite normal. If someone approached me in those days and told me I was acting oddly, I would think they were wrong and that they were attacking me. They didn't get it; they didn't get me. This is because my trauma-informed view of the world created a belief within me that felt as real as any other bodily need or desire. When I am hungry, for example, I feel that and know that. If someone were to come up to me and tell me that I was not actually hungry, I would trust my mind, body, and feelings over their words. Trauma is just like that. As my body and mind would be reacting to a trigger I had not yet come to recognize, warning me of a danger that did not actually exist, I would suddenly seem rather angry or irrational.

Trauma holds memories in our body, and a smell or sound or any number of things can trigger that response. At that point, we are just along for the ride until we know how to untangle from the mess. As Dr. Bessel A. van der Kolk says in his wonderful book *The Body Keeps the Score*, "In order to change, people need to become aware of their sensations and the way that their bodies interact with the world around them. Physical self-awareness is the first step in releasing the tyranny of the past."

For me, achieving this awareness was challenging. Sometimes when I encountered a trigger, I would be so busy trying to cope with the symptoms that I couldn't pay attention to what was happening inside of me. As a result, it could feel as though the world around me had gone mad. People were rude and overstepping boundaries and driving foolishly, and what the heck did that cashier mean by that last statement, and why are people taking so long to do anything? Those types of days are wonderful warnings for me. It is unlikely that all the people I'm coming in contact with are the problem when the only constant in those interactions is me. On days like that, I can now recognize that I need to step back and take a long hard look at what I am doing—and more importantly, what have I been doing within the last week or so—so that I can recognize where all these feelings are coming from.

In order to make this change, I spent years in counselling learning to recognize the impact of trauma and the signs that I was falling into a victim mentality. I learned to recognize

One tool that I have found helpful for understanding why we behave in certain ways and for creating healthier relationships is the Karpman Drama Triangle. This is a model that shows the connection between personal responsibility and power in conflicts as well as the roles people play within them. These roles are the Victim, the Rescuer, and the Persecutor.

the extremes in my thought patterns—for instance, making statements like "always" and "never," which left no room for conversations, forgiveness, and other perspectives. This way of seeing the world, along with my experiences, was keeping me trapped in my role as the victim even when I did not recognize that and would have been angry at anyone who suggested such a thing. It took time and healing to realize that I needed to change my internal narrative away from extremes and blaming and harshness. I needed to find a way of thinking that would allow me to heal, to really look at what I wanted in life, and to communicate that to myself and to the people around me.

One tool that I have found helpful for understanding why we behave in certain ways and for creating healthier relationships is the Karpman Drama Triangle. This is a model that shows the connection between personal responsibility and power in conflicts as well as the roles people play within them. These roles are the Victim, the Rescuer, and the Persecutor. In their extreme versions, the Victim is played by a person who feels they are being wrongly blamed or unfairly treated. They refuse to take responsibility for their circumstances and deny that they have any power to change them. The Rescuer is the person that bails the Victim out of their difficulties, takes their side, and confirms for them that they are, in fact, a victim. They are an enabler who relies on helping others as a way to feel good about themselves. The Persecutor is the person who criticizes and blames the victim, sometimes to the point of bullying, in an effort to avoid becoming a victim themselves. They can be controlling, rigid, and authoritative, but they don't actually help anyone solve their problems.

While these extreme versions are the most recognizable, we will often come across people playing milder versions of these roles, perhaps as a result of their own trauma. We will also likely play one or more of these roles ourselves. An important note is that people do not stay stuck in one of these roles; they may cycle through all three of them without ever getting out of the triangle.

In order to take back our own power, we need to stand back and look at our own part in these conflicts. And once we do that, we can flip these roles on their heads. The Victim can become the Creator, looking for ways to change their situation. The Rescuer can become the Challenger, stand by the Creator and encouraging them to move forward. The Prosecutor can become the Coach, listening and responding to the Creator and suggesting new methods to try.

Self-awareness does not just stop at recognizing how trauma shows up in our lives. In order to heal, we also need to learn to recognize the triggers that bring on these symptoms. And sometimes, recognizing our triggers can be more complicated than we might expect.

8

Triggers Can Be Sneaky

"Being traumatized means continuing to organize your life as if the trauma were still going on—unchanged and immutable—as every new encounter or event is contaminated by the past."
Bessel A. van der Kolk, *The Body Keeps the Score: Brain, Mind, and Body in the Healing of Trauma*

Some days, trauma barges in like an irate drunk, leaving a trail of destruction in its path. As abusive and intrusive as this feels, there is some comfort in the fact that we at least recognize it—the smells, sounds, and sensations are familiar and easily spotted.

Some days, though, trauma sneaks in through a back entrance. Slithering in like a snake, we are completely unsuspecting of its presence until it springs and sinks its fangs into us. The toxins are rushing through our body before we have a moment to recoil, and we are left feeling re-traumatized, shocked, and vulnerable.

Some of my triggers can be very obvious to me. A rape scene in a movie or TV show, especially a graphic one, can result in days of feeling off balance if I don't take control of it. A picture of an abused animal on social media could take me days to let go of. I must always be diligent. I do my best to be conscious of what I'm watching and looking at, and I know to turn off the show or step away from the computer if something becomes too much. On the flip side, I find that shows that include justice being served are particularly good for me. I can watch a rather graphic movie if there is some kind of punishment being handed out to the bad guys—a wrong made right somehow. This is a far cry from the forgiveness I so strongly believe in, yet there is still some place within me that longs for justice in a world that feels rather unjust at times.

Most of the time, though, my triggers liked to be sneaky. Seemingly out of nowhere, I would suddenly find myself experiencing a variety of symptoms—perhaps a headache, a stomach ache, a racing heart, terror, anxiety, nausea, or dizziness. It never occurred to me in those days and moments that the situation, place, smell, sound, or whatever sensory or situational stimulus was present might be reminding me of a traumatic event.

One day, my daughter, who was about seventeen or eighteen years old at the time, required dental surgery. It was simple day surgery, so my job was to drive her there, help her with the preparation process, and then drive her home at the end of it. Jessie has some cognitive challenges, so she required some extra supports to make this all work for her and help her understand what was happening. Developmentally, she was closer to twelve years old at that time. As is not uncommon for a person who struggles to process the world around her, she had a tendency to say she understands something even if she doesn't. She is also lovely and wonderful and polite, so people don't always notice her cognitive challenges right away.

The moment we walked into the hospital, I became very disoriented; I started to hyperventilate a little bit, and swallowing became very difficult. I didn't know what was happening. It never occurred to me that I was being triggered; it felt like I was having an allergic reaction. I was there to support my daughter, though, so I did my best to hide the fact that I was struggling. She was the one going in for surgery; she shouldn't have to calm me down.

We got to where Jessie needed to check in, and the person who was taking her information seemed confused as to why I was assisting her. This caused a moment of tension when the nurse insisted that Jessie should be able to answer questions on her own—triggers can often make us overly sensitive, and my response was perhaps not as gently worded as it could have been. Thankfully we were able to clear up the miscommunication, and then it was time for Jess to go in.

As I waited for the surgery to finish, I began wandering around the hospital. It was quite early in the morning, so the building was still kind of dark in some places. Suddenly, I start to panic. I was filled with a sense that something horrible was going to happen, and I had an irrational yet overwhelming desire to stop the surgery. This feeling was as strong as if I was watching a car about to run my daughter over. It came in like a cyclone and tore me apart on the inside, and I was alone, terrified, and completely unprepared. I began crying and hyperventilating, and I could not figure out what was going on inside of me.

What had started with me wondering if I was having a mild allergic reaction had escalated into what was going to be a scene from the movie *Taken*. I have a particular set of skills, and if you don't let me get my daughter out of here right now, you are about to feel the weight of all of them come crashing down upon you.

In that moment, I decided to call my friend Judy, for whom I am so grateful. I can't tell you how I knew to call someone, or even how I was able to use a phone—this back in the days of payphones. We talked for a while, which consisted mostly of me swearing and sweating and crying and ranting while she listened, so kind and gentle. And somehow, we unravelled the mess together. She helped me see that this was the first time I had taken my precious daughter into a hospital since the surgery to repair the damage from when she was raped over a decade earlier.

I had no warning this was coming. I was not thinking of that horrible time in our lives when we arrived at the hospital; I was simply taking her to have some teeth pulled and a retainer removed. Trauma was silently waiting in the darkened corners of the hospital that morning, patient, cruel, and powerful.

Another time, about twenty years ago, I was going through a period when I was struggling, really struggling. My husband Dave, who is in the Navy, had been deployed. I was very used to him being away and usually handled deployments quite well, but this time was different. There had been things coming up from my past, memories I wasn't dealing with because they came up one at a time and I wasn't really paying attention. Jessie was getting married and there were fears around all of that. Would she be happy? Would she be safe? No one thing was an issue on its own, but each one was piling on top of the other.

Quite suddenly, things took a turn. I stopped leaving the house. I was losing weight in a really unhealthy way, burning calories through sheer nerves and terror on top of not eating well. I was having a lot of abdominal pain, and my bowels were impacted for quite some time. One doctor even told me that if we couldn't get it sorted out soon, they may have to consider surgery. I was in and out of the hospital and was in a constant state of anxiety. I decided that I probably had cancer or something equally horrible; once again, it never occurred to me that my mind was attacking me.

All the while, my friend Nigel, who was one of the chaplains at the base, was seeing what I could not. He offered to request that Dave be sent home, and I remember saying to him, "Don't you dare tell Dave what is going on here! He has enough going on!" I thought that if this did turn out to be cancer, I was really going to need him then. I also didn't want him to be seen as the guy with the crazy wife. My inner voice was unkind and full of judgement and shame—this is one sure way to recognize when trauma is visiting. The way I spoke to myself was so abusive; I would never have allowed anyone I cared about to be spoken to in that way.

Eventually I went to see my doctor, who quickly recognized what was going on. He referred me to another doctor who specialized in PTSD. I was so resistant at first—this was the first time this diagnosis had been suggested to me, and I wasn't sure I agreed with it. My doctor kindly and gently told me that he had seen this before, where things seem to "suddenly" bubble up, and that it wouldn't hurt to see someone who really understood how to help a person in this type of situation. He referred me to Dr. Malcolm, a psychologist who worked with many military personnel with PTSD and was very experienced in helping people recover from trauma.

When Dave returned after six months away, I was still not doing well. He was really shaken that all this was happening while he was gone and I never shared any of it. He said, "This isn't a dishwasher that isn't working properly! You are my wife, and you were in the hospital possibly facing surgery and you didn't tell me!" It was another example of how I still felt at times that I needed to keep things secret; thankfully, we were able to sort through that part.

One day, shortly after Dave was home, he suggested that we go for a drive so that I could get out of the house. We drove along the water for a while, then went along a beautiful country road I had never been on before. As we were driving, I suddenly became filled with unexplainable terror. I started screaming at Dave, demanding that he get me away from there. "Why would you take me here? Why would you do this to me? Get me out of here!" Overwhelmed by fear, my language was accusing and unkind.

Dave pulled a U-turn in the middle of the road and started taking me home as quickly as he could. The whole time I was sobbing and screaming at him, accusing him of doing that

Triggers can be tricky. They don't announce themselves; we just find ourselves suddenly filled with terror, and we react without questioning. Unlearning the nervous system's response to trauma, along with understanding how triggers and trauma feel in our body, is an important part to finding our way out of this cycle.

on purpose. But what had he done? Even I wasn't fully aware of what was happening. I can tell you that Dave certainly did not, nor would he ever, intentionally do anything to bring harm to me in any way. There is nothing he wouldn't do to protect me, and to have me ranting and raving and accusing him broke his heart.

I called Dr. Malcolm as soon as we got home, still in hysterics, and this wonderful man cancelled his appointments and saw me immediately so that we could make some sense of what had just happened. He was so kind and so patient. Over the course of a few hours, he helped me see what he had known from the moment I called him: that I had just experienced a major trigger, and since I was already not doing well, I had nothing left in me to cope with it.

Dave took me for a drive that was lovely and needed and should have been a great distraction, but the road that we were driving on looked very much like the road I had been taken down by one of my rapists. It was not *the* road—we live on Vancouver Island while the assault occurred on the mainland—but it looked similar enough that I became disoriented and confused, and I completely lost where I was. Without me realizing it, I was immediately transported to the actual, life-threatening, terrifying trauma, and that is the intensity with which I reacted.

Triggers can be tricky. They don't announce themselves; we just find ourselves suddenly filled with terror, and we react without questioning. Unlearning the nervous system's response to trauma, along with understanding how triggers and trauma feel in our body, is an important part to finding our way out of this cycle.

Dancing Crow by Alison Perry-Davies

A mixed media piece I created as I was processing my heart breaking over losing music. I left it outside to dry and a crow stepped into the plaster and danced across the painting. It made it beautiful to me and gave me hope.

9

Living with Intention

"True life is lived when tiny changes occur."
Leo Tolstoy

O nce I better understood where I was, I began to look at where I wanted to be. That vision became a path, a map, a goal. We've all been told that if we can dream it, we can have it, but that does not happen simply by dreaming. Our path to healing and wholeness comes with a decision to live with intention.

When I was trapped in a life filled with anguish, resentment, and bitterness, I could see the life I wanted yet it seemed unattainable. That life was way over there somewhere, and I was over here without any clue as to how to bridge the cavernous gap. I couldn't even see that I was in a prison of my own making, and once I did, I was so filled with trauma and grief and pain that I could not see a way out.

Many of us have built such a prison within ourselves, and escaping it is no small feat. If, through some well-organized plan, we were able to sneak out, the cell would still be there, waiting for us. If we used dynamite to blow a hole in the side, there would still be rubble. We need to completely dismantle that cell so there is no place to return to. We need to take apart the prison brick by brick—bricks of shame and pain that spin and twist our memories so deeply that we can't catch our balance. This is a slow process. It took a very long time to build that prison, so it isn't about to come down in one day or even one year.

We also need to remove the charges against us or else we can still be trapped, imprisoned, caged. We need to be pardoned or exonerated for what we have done, or for what has been done to us. We have to take the claws out of our side that twist and turn and hold us back. We need to find a way to heal; for me, that meant finding a way to forgive.

There is no finish line in the journey of healing from trauma. Instead, there are layers of recovery, layers of healing, that come one step at a time. As we search for ways of coping and managing our traumas, we trip and fall and then we get back up.

TRIGGERS

As I mentioned before, one of the first steps in my journey was learning to recognize my triggers even before they happened. For years I worked with Dr. Malcolm—along with other doctors, therapists, and complementary wellness practitioners—to learn this important skill, though the lessons didn't always make sense at the time. As I moved through the layers of healing, things started to make sense and something I had learned ten or twenty years earlier would suddenly come alive. A seed had been planted, and after years of pulling up weeds and fertilizing the garden, it started to grow.

I learned that when triggers occurred, I first needed to take a step back and use breathing and relaxation techniques to avoid becoming overwhelmed. Then, I needed to use the tools I had available in order to centre myself and become aware of my surroundings so that I could identify what was triggering me. Developing these skills gave me the ability to recognize a trigger before it happened and to prepare myself for potential triggers when I was going into a situation. This was a game changer and allowed me to start living and enjoying life, perhaps for the first time.

Another step was finding ways to unplug myself from "terror tsunamis," as I call them. These are overwhelming moments, like my experience in the hospital with Jess or the drive with David, and they were becoming more and more frequent. Creativity was helping me manage my day-to-day emotions, but what I needed was to find a way to stop the tsunami from completely overtaking me.

One wonderful tool for breaking ourselves out of an anxiety attack or a trigger is called grounding. There are several different ways to approach this method, but the first step is always to find our breath. When we are in the midst of a "terror attack," the first thing that typically goes out of control is our breathing. We begin to hyperventilate and become dizzy or light-headed, which makes it much more difficult to centre ourselves and regain self-control.

GROUNDING

Start by taking a slow, deep breath in for a count of however many seconds is comfortable for you—ideally three to five, but if you can only manage one or two then just focus on that. Hold at the top of your breath for that same amount of time, and then release for that same amount as well. It can be difficult at first as your mind is racing and adrenaline is pumping. As you continue to take slow, relaxing breaths, though, they should become easier to do.

Once your breathing is under control, then you can use the "rule of five" to help ground yourself. Look around your environment and go through these five steps:

- Acknowledge FIVE things you see around you.
- Acknowledge FOUR things you can touch around you.
- Acknowledge THREE things you hear around you.
- Acknowledge TWO things you can smell around you.
- Acknowledge ONE thing you can taste.

CONTROLLED TRIGGERS

Another useful tool that Dr. Malcolm shared with me is controlled triggers: finding a way to bring on a trigger in a controlled manner, and then using that to learn ways to bring myself to a place of peace and calm. And so that's what I did. I would either go to a place or revisit a memory that would trigger me—sometimes on my own, sometimes with the help of Dr. Malcom—and then I would tell myself, "This is not where you are now. It's not what's happening now. Look around you." And then I would do something to ground myself and bring myself back to what was really happening. I would touch a table. I would pinch myself. I would look at five things in the room and identify them. Eventually, I was able to get to a place where if I encountered a trigger, I would be able to recognize it and remind myself what was really happening—that whatever this terror response was, it wasn't required right now. It had kept me safe. It had kept me alive. But right now, it wasn't helping. And then I would return to those grounding exercises.

Acknowledge FIVE things you see around you.
Acknowledge FOUR things you can touch around you.
Acknowledge THREE things you hear around you.
Acknowledge TWO things you can smell around you.
Acknowledge ONE thing you can taste.

I once had an experience with my brother Jamie that served as a gentle reminder of the power of self-soothing words. When our dad was in hospice, the two of us would spend the night with him and have long conversations. We'd been spending as much time with him as possible, and as beautiful as it all was, I was pushing beyond what my new brain was capable of handling and my energy was depleted. Those are always the times when a trauma would find its way back into my psyche. One particular evening, Jamie and I were talking about something, I don't recall what exactly, and I started to become triggered. Jamie—who is a very wise old soul—observed me for a bit and then said, "It's okay, everyone is safe. That's not what's happening now. You don't need to be afraid."

Hearing these words deeply calmed me. I was amazed that my brother intuitively knew to say what I had been telling myself all these years.

Speaking light into darkness is a beautifully powerful way to bring healing. If we are walking down a dark trail and turn a flashlight on, the trail no longer seems so treacherous. Similarly, I have found that when a simple truth is spoken in the midst of a trauma trigger, it unplugs us from the energy source that would like to drag us into the darkness.

Trauma wants us to see ourselves as victims—if it can keep us trapped in that role, it is very difficult for us to move forward. It creates drama and exaggerations in situations that are already so difficult to process. It's just like what we see happening with social media. There is what is actually happening—an election, a pandemic, any number of events in the world— and then there's the drama that swirls around it, picks at it, expands on one area and over-exaggerates another, all to make it seem so out of control. It is unnecessary, unkind, and not at all part of any healthy solution. When you notice this happening, it's really good to turn on the light, speak truth into the darkness, and unplug the energy source that is feeding all the drama.

I have also found that understanding what is physically happening inside of me—my brain, my body, my emotions, my spirit—during times when I am triggered is very important as it helps me to figure out what I can do to counter those responses. Guided relaxation breathing has been so helpful for checking in with my body and being aware of it so that I can relax and let go of the tension I so often hold in all of my muscles. As the calming voice in my breathing tape says: breathe in calm, positive energy and release all tension and worry. OHM.

OTHER TECHNIQUES

So much of what we enjoy and do naturally has a wonderful impact on our health, specifically mental health. For example, walking every day, even for just thirty minutes, is really important for me—for all of us, actually. It is a wonderful, gentle way to move our bodies. This is especially beneficial in today's world, with so many people working in offices and sitting for hours each day.

Through my studies of psychology, counselling, and holistic wellness, I learned why I felt better when I went for walks. Just as chronic anxiety and stress release excess hormones that wreak havoc on our physical and mental wellbeing, exercise (and walking, specifically) releases chemicals called endorphins that serve as natural painkillers and mood enhancers. For this reason, being physically active reduces our risk of depression by thirty percent and can help those who are already depressed to recover.

Over the years, my dear friend Glenn and I have shared many conversations and ideas around different methods of healing. He was a neuro-linguistic programming (NLP) practitioner, and he taught me about EFT tapping, which involves tapping on different parts of the body to help balance energy and reduce physical and emotional pain. I was so very skeptical at first, but one day we did a session together, and then I headed off to run some errands. For the next four hours, I had to stop to pee about every thirty minutes—and I am talking going like I had been drinking beer all night or something. It was clear to me that something had shifted and released, and this was physical evidence of that fact. I have found tapping to be very effective and continue to explore it with Glenn as my guide.

I also love to find beautiful, healthy distractions that put me in a good mood. One such distraction is The Graham Norton Show, a British talk show that is—in my mind—the standard all other shows should aim for. The host is delightful and cheeky, and he has such amazing chemistry with the guests. His show can take me from a dark place to absolute full-on belly laughter in minutes, and it is one of my all-time favourite therapies. Studies have shown that laughter releases those feel-good endorphins, as well as dopamine and serotonin which have a similar effect. I love to laugh!

Getting enough sleep is another important aspect. I aim for six to eight hours a night and do my best to get to bed by 10:00 p.m. There is a pharmacist in my community, Dr. Gerry Poon, who also trained in homeopathic and Chinese medicines before earning a PhD in restorative medicine, and he has been a wealth of information for me. One thing I learned from him is that we get our regenerative sleep—a deep sleep which supports healing— between 10:00 p.m. and 2:00 a.m., so I follow his advice and try to be asleep during that time.

On that note, I suggest looking for the treasures in your community! I have found that most communities have people within them who are amazing resources. This might be a doctor, a librarian, a pharmacist, a friend, or even someone's nana—anyone who is known to be a wealth of information and is willing to share their knowledge with others. Some people offer this information for free, and for those who do charge a fee, there is often a way to work out a sliding scale if you are truly unable to pay. I spent years as a single working mum with a very limited budget, and I found that if I was looking for ways to help myself and my kids, I could usually figure out a way to move forward.

I have taken so many paths on my journey to healing, and I am so grateful that one of them led me to John and Paula Sandford of Elijah House and their teachings on forgiveness, on understanding how we curse ourselves and others, and on making vows. Their Christian-based counselling model and way of looking at how much judgement and resentment I was holding on to without realizing it, brought me much relief and helped to bring healing to my entire family.

Part of this process was remembering the judgements and vows I had made back when I was little, frightened Alison, alone and in pain. I had to examine all the times I had said to myself "I would never do that" or "I will never let anyone leave me again." I had to pay attention to how I had judged my dad or my mum or anyone else in my life. Those vows and judgements had shaped my choices, connecting and creating a pattern of similar behaviours. For me, much of my healing came through learning to forgive those who had hurt me and my children as well as learning to forgive myself for the ways I felt I had fallen short. Through the teachings of Elijah House, I was able to let go of some of the judgements and anger I had held on to so tightly.

One healing method we used to help release myself of these judgements is where a person stands in the stead of the one who caused you harm or pain and asks you for forgiveness on their behalf. In this way, you can face the person without them being there. It was very powerful for me, and it helped me to change that unhealthy pattern in my life.

Unravelling our traumas and finding ways to be healthier is a lot like untangling Christmas lights. We have to be careful and focussed on looking for the best way, the safest way, to unravel the mess. Some of us might wrap that string of lights around a piece of cardboard to ensure they don't become tangled up again; others might become rushed and wrap them around their arm a few times, then shove them in a storage tub and forget about them until next year.

Despite our best efforts, sometimes we pull them out and discover they are once again all jumbled up. How the heck did that happen? Who goes on in there and messes with this stuff? The truth is that no one does; it just happens. Things shift and move and become tangled without us being aware of it.

I have found that healing our mind, heart, and spirit is much like that. We do not "untangle the lights" once and then be done with it forever. If we want to remain untangled, we will need to continually care for our emotional, mental, physical, and spiritual wellbeing. We will need to live with intention and keep moving forward, one step at a time. We need to dismantle the prison we have built around ourselves so that we can truly be free.

When Peace Comes
by Alison Perry-Davies

This was a layer by layer
somatic process of mixed media
using clay and beads gifted to
me by a friend.

10

Guarding My Gates

"Only when we are brave enough to explore the darkness will we discover the infinite power of our light."
Brené Brown

When I was in my early twenties, I "suddenly" developed some allergies and sensitivities. I spoke with an allergy specialist, and he told me to imagine that my body was a bag of water. Stressors go into it drip by drip until the bag reaches its limit and bursts. A person can only take so much; eventually the body, the mind, the spirit, the emotions, the person will break. In my case, some of this manifested as allergies and sensitivities to a number of things, such as some foods and scents. These all started while we were going through the process of surgeries and legal proceedings after Jess' assault, and yet it hadn't occurred to me that there was a connection. This is one example of how important it is to take care of our body, mind, emotions, and spirit while recovering from trauma.

The twelve-step programs have a wonderful little acronym, HALT, which stands for Hungry, Angry, Lonely, and Tired. The premise is that life will do what life does. There will be unexpected bills, toothaches, distracted drivers, and rude people in shopping malls. In those times, if we are already dealing with being hungry, angry, lonely, or tired, we may handle these inconveniences in a way that we might regret. When we find ourselves struggling to cope, we can use the HALT acronym as a reminder to pause and assess if any of these are the cause.

In a similar vein, I have found an approach to self-care that is very important for my overall wellbeing. I need to take a higher level of responsibility for myself than perhaps other people do, yet it doesn't take much for things to go right. I only require some consistency, a rhythm. To achieve this, I have to be very aware of what I call my gates: my eyes, my ears, my mouth, and my mind. They are the guardians of what I let into—and sometimes out of—my body, and they serve an important role in helping me manage my triggers and trauma.

EYE GATES

My eye gates control what I see, watch, and read. Over the years I have learned to be aware of what I am exposing myself to throughout my day and how it may impact me. Once we see something, we cannot "unsee" it.

There are a lot of wonderful things to see in the media, but there is also so much negativity, especially on social media. Politics, opinions, conspiracy theories, more information than we can possibly take in are all presented to us faster than we can process it or form an informed opinion for ourselves. Who has the time to research every single theory that is blasted at us? And even if we did have the time, would we want to? It is a constant barrage of often very angry and emotional people, ideas, and opinions, and it will eat us whole if we allow it to.

I also need to be conscious of the shows and movies to which I expose myself. To be clear, I am talking about personal censorship—what does not work well for me might be fine for someone else. Graphic rape scenes and animals being hurt, especially dogs, are both triggers for me, so I do my best to avoid media that includes those kinds of scenes. If I encounter one when I am at home watching a show, I will mute that scene and fast forward through it or choose not to watch that show at all. I get that these are sometimes part of the story they are trying to tell, but I just don't need to see it.

EAR GATES

The next are my ear gates, which I have already somewhat gone over in the previous paragraph. At our house, we use the mute button a lot. I also have to be very careful with lyrics; it is easy for me to get into a rhythm of a song and then realize that the lyrics are not something I want in my life. It isn't necessarily that the lyrics are graphic or violent, nor is it that they involve a political or social justice ideology I am avoiding. Sometimes, the lyrics just create feelings that I don't want, and so I will switch to something else.

Songs may also trigger me if they played while a traumatic event occurred. I used to try to force myself to listen and take control over the feelings; I didn't honour the place in me that told me it hurt or made me uncomfortable. Now, I listen to my body and my emotions, and if a song or sound has a negative impact and I don't see any value in desensitizing myself to it, I simply remove it. It is all about listening to the place within me that understands what works for me and what doesn't.

MOUTH GATE

My mouth controls what I eat, what I drink, and what I say. Personally, I find I need to eat well and drink lots of water. For me, this means choosing "clean" foods and being very aware of ingredients that I am allergic or sensitive to. There were certainly times in my life when I couldn't afford to eat only organic foods, and during those times I was careful to eat as healthy as I could. I also really listen to what my body is telling me about which foods make me feel better and which foods don't sit well.

I also do my best to support local farms and businesses. I find that generally following the 100-mile diet, which encourages us to shop and eat from more local sources, allows me to buy healthier produce as well as building and being a part of my community. These small steps create a sense of wellbeing and balance, and that is where I thrive—and thriving is how I want to live.

In addition to paying attention to what goes in my mouth, I also need to be careful of what comes out of it. Between my brain injury and my PTSD, my filter is not always what I would like it to be. I am recovered enough to sit and have a wonderful conversation with you, but sometimes I share more or less than I intend to. I suppose the silver lining in all of this is that with my new brain, I might not always remember when I talk about something a little more personal than I would like.

There are times when we need to unload some of what we carry. I have found that in these situations, it is best that I am careful about what I share. I don't want to traumatize someone else, and parts of my story can be triggers for others who have had similar experiences.

Finding a person or a few people who I can trust and who have some understanding of my experiences is important for me. People are not perfect. We hurt each other—sometimes mistakenly, sometimes intentionally—and the best way to limit that pain is to be kind and to connect with other like-minded people. For friends and professionals alike, it is important to find people we feel safe with. If it doesn't feel right, trust your gut. Even if what we are picking up is due to our own issues and not about them at all, it is better to honour our feelings. Many of us have had that level of control taken from us, and part of our healing journey can be taking that power back.

MIND GATE

The last gate is my mind gate, which oversees what I allow myself to think about. One of the things that people with trauma and people with brain injuries have in common—and perhaps even people with obsessive thoughts or OCD—is something I refer to as a "loop." In musical terms, a loop can be used when a musician records a sound and plays it over and over while they play other notes on top of that. This is particularly useful for people who are making music on their own as it helps to add more dimension and sound to whatever they are playing. For example, I might create a loop for a drum pattern, and then another loop of some guitar chords, and then I play my keyboard on top of that.

A looping thought is somewhat similar: a thought comes into my head, usually what would be referred to as an intrusive thought, and it plays over and over. It could be a good thought, but typically they feel negative. These loops are more likely to occur when I have not been eating well, sleeping well, exercising, and getting fresh air. They can also occur when I am not as mindful about my other gates as I should be and allow in something negative or triggering. Loops can be very difficult to derail and can lead to behaviours like isolating, unhealthy eating, distracting myself with social media, and all kinds of things that are counterproductive to achieving peace, balance, and joy.

One approach that can help redirect these thoughts is playing or singing an upbeat, happy song with a great message. I've created a playlist I can go through in these moments so that I don't have to come up with a song on the spot. One of my favourites is Redbone's "Come and Get Your Love"—I can loop that for some time, and it is often what I play in my head as I fall asleep. Another is "Life Is Sweet," written by Bocephus King (who happens to be my brother). It is so lovely and simple and takes me to a sunny place. This is another way in which creativity washes over me and pulls me out of the dark places.

Since my accident, taking control of my thoughts has become more important than ever. My brain now physically buzzes when I get tired or overdo things. Have you ever put your tongue on a battery to see if it still has power? You know that little buzzy feeling that happens once your tongue makes contact? When I get tired or do just about any activity for too long, I get that exact feeling in my brain. And although it has been over six years since my car accident, it still unsettles me, and I still go away by myself and cry sometimes because I just want it to stop.

I tend to be a visionary type; it is just how my mind works. I always want to see how I can do things differently. I want to add an ingredient that completely changes the recipe. I love to play around with old things to make them new—my own interpretation of what was. I want to play a song with just enough of the melody that it is somewhat recognizable, surprising the listener once they realize what I've done with the arrangement. It isn't so much that I think outside the box, I just haven't quite figured out that there *is* a box. Besides, I'm claustrophobic; boxes and I don't get along so well.

In contrast, I have wonderful, fabulous friends who tend to be more linear in their processing. They follow those neat straight lines, and their lives are very much in order. It is a beautiful thing. They are great at taking one step at a time. They find one thing to clean, maybe a drawer, instead of an entire room. They pick one task on their to-do list instead of getting lost in how much needs to be done. They take their time, choose a task, and follow through. If they need a break, they take one. As I get older and my way of thinking gets healthier, I can see some of the wisdom in this approach, and I've even started trying to follow some of their ways.

So, for today, I will not get overwhelmed by all the "shoulds" and "coulds." It is easy for me to look at the things I want or need to do and begin to panic, receiving a wave of negative self-talk from the inner critic that is so far beyond what is healthy. Those of us with unhealed trauma live with a nonstop bully in our head that berates and criticizes and threatens and accuses, making it almost impossible to complete the slightest task. You see, we aren't just looking at something that needs to be done, like a room that needs to get cleaned or a drawer that should be organized. First, we have to deal with a barrage of self-induced cruelty and name calling. And if that wasn't energy sucking enough, we also have to work to hide those thoughts so that no one would ever suspect all that is happening inside us. Keeping our secrets is of utmost importance, and until we can get to the place where we can silence those attacks from inside ourselves, everything else is so much more challenging. It's like instead of walking up stairs, we go and grab a 100-pound backpack and put on roller skates, and *then* we try to ascend.

Time, healing, and recognizing those unwanted and unsolicited thoughts helps us to remove these additional challenges we have placed on ourselves—the accusations and the secrets—and just walk up the stairs the way stairs were intended to be walked up. We must find our way to healing, and then it is crucial that we stay on top of it and check in with ourselves regularly.

ENERGY

One more thing I must be aware of that doesn't neatly fit into these gates is energy. Energy may be invisible to our eyes, but certainly not the rest of our senses. Think about watching the wind blow while you are sitting inside of your house—even though the wind itself is invisible, its impact is not. Trees bend, grass moves; a strong enough wind once pulled our BBQ off the porch and down the stairs. Similarly, many of us have walked into a room to find a couple sitting there smiling, yet there is a palpable tension. Before we have really seen their glances or even noticed their body language, we perceive a heaviness in the air.

I was a passenger in a motor vehicle accident one time, and our car was hit right on the passenger door. The vehicle we were in had protective barriers built in along the sides, which meant there was very little damage to our vehicle compared to what would have happened if the car was older. This barrier stopped the other car from ripping through us; instead, as

Whatever name one might give this sense—whether it be intuition or clairvoyance or simply being observant —it is nothing new.
I have learned that I need to step back and ask myself if whatever I'm feeling is my own or something I am sensing that is not mine to carry.

a doctor explained it to me, that energy continued through everything it came upon, our bodies included. So, while we were spared broken bones and torn flesh—which is wonderful— the energy still travelled through our bodies and the soft tissue damage was more intense. Invisible, powerful energy.

This phenomenon can be seen throughout our lives. A person walks into a room, joyful and full of light and life, and soon everyone around them feels a little better. The opposite can be true; an angry person can stir anger in others, or a person that is feeling very depressed and dark can share that energy as well.

This knowledge has given me a theory about the rate of storage units in North America. They are everywhere these days; this was not the case years ago. People are consuming, buying, and collecting so much stuff that we have to build a place specifically to store it. Meanwhile, all around us there are people who are truly in need. They do not have food or water or shelter, and their spirits, their voices, their very beings cry out. Even if they never utter a word, their existence on this shared planet cries out. And I suspect that around the world, this energy lands on millions of people, many of whom are unaware of this invisible energy and mistake it for their own. We try to fill that need, that void, without recognizing what is driving us. We continue to consume until our house is full, and then we consume some more and put it into a storage unit. Storage units absolutely have their place in the world, but I wonder if there isn't some connection between overconsumption and so many of us feeling this need energetically and mistakenly believing that it is our own.

Whatever name one might give this sense—whether it be intuition or clairvoyance or simply being observant—it is nothing new. I have learned that I need to step back and ask myself if whatever I'm feeling is my own or something I am sensing that is not mine to carry. The best way to achieve this is to ask myself how my feelings came about and where they were first initiated.

Through social media, we can see how different people respond to, react to, and process many emotions, thoughts, and ideas. This has been especially true during the COVID-19 pandemic, with so many people facing enormous challenges and a constant stream of new information being thrown our way. How many of these thoughts or feelings actually originated or were initiated by the person, and how many were caused by the emotion and energy we are all processing without even being aware of it? The energy swirls like the wind, and until we see the tree branches move or the BBQ fly off the porch, we might not be aware of how powerful that energy is.

Whenever I think I am being impacted by the energy around me, I need to step back, disconnect from anything or anyone that might influence my thoughts and emotions, practice meditation, go for a walk, paint, write, sing, whatever I need to do to centre myself again. Then, if I need to process information, I can do that with a cleaner slate.

When I pay attention to my gates and to the energy around me, I am able to find much more peace, balance, and joy in my life. So, I will watch and read and look at things that are a positive influence on me. I will speak to myself more kindly. I will eat healthier so that my brain and body have a chance to sustain me. I will find a way to do some form of exercise daily. I will pay attention to the energy surrounding me. I will give myself a chance to succeed.

11

You Are What You Think

"Thoughts don't become things; thoughts ARE things."
Eric Micha'el Leventhal

My friend Glenn told me once that my innate creativity might be the reason I have so much anxiety. The same vivid imagination that allows me to write a song, paint a picture, or write a book dreams up all sorts of possible outcomes, many of which can sometimes scare me. I have a collection of children's books coming out soon, and one of them discusses making sure we guide our imagination and not just let it go wherever it wants to. To explain this concept, I use the analogy of our feet as it seemed to be something kids would understand. I talk about how we don't just let our feet go anywhere they like, because then they might take us out in traffic or off a cliff. Instead, we tell them where we want to go. Imaginations are much like that—they can take us on great adventures or into dark and scary places, so we need to be sure that we are guiding it in the right direction.

For so long, my anxiety held me prisoner. I always wanted to be the adventurous type—the kind of person who really squeezes every possible bit of enjoyment and exploration out of life. Instead, I was often paralyzed by the "what ifs," daydreaming about all that could have and should have been. My mind would be either worried about all that could go wrong and had already gone wrong in my young life, or it would be lost in a make-believe world where I could do and be anything. Part of my journey has been really paying attention to my thoughts and my words as well as being willing to challenge myself and direct where I allow my mind to wander.

A few decades ago, I took a course that taught how to listen and understand the different ways God or creation itself speaks to us. During that course, I was introduced to the experiments done by Masaru Emoto. Emoto said that water was a "blueprint for our reality" and that emotional "energies" and "vibrations" could actually change the physical structure of water. To prove this, he set up experiments that consisted of exposing water in glasses to different words, pictures, or music. Sometimes he placed labels on the glasses, some with positive words or phrases and others with negative ones. Sometimes he would have people speak the words over the glasses. Some glasses were ignored. At the end of the experiment, he would freeze the glasses of water and examine the aesthetic properties of the crystals with microscopic photography.

The findings were dramatic. The glasses with negative phrases, along with the ones that were ignored, had crystals that were dark and blurry looking. In contrast, the glasses with positive words and phrases were beautiful works of crystallized art.

At this point, you may be wondering why this matters. Who cares if glasses of water like to be talked to nicely? Well, according to the *Journal of Biological Chemistry*, up to sixty percent of the adult human body is water. So, knowing what can happen with water in a glass, imagine the impact that words and thoughts can have on our body, mind, spirit, and emotions.

Of course, this concept is nothing new—many great teachers and prophets have taught of the power of our words and thoughts. In the Old Testament of the Bible, Proverbs 23:7 says, "As a man thinks, so is he." Similarly, Philippians 4:8 in the New Testament declares, "Finally, brothers, whatever is true, whatever is honorable, whatever is just, whatever is pure, whatever is lovely, whatever is commendable, if there is any excellence, if there is anything worthy of praise, think about these things." These passages remind us to have control over our thoughts and think on things that would bring us life.

Such teachings can be found outside of the Bible as well. Buddha once described the mind as a wild horse. In the Eightfold Path, he recommends practicing "right effort" by first avoiding and then clearing our minds of negative, unwholesome thoughts. Once that is achieved, we can attain a wholesome, tranquil state of mind through the practice of positive thinking.

It seems to me that much like the algorithms on social media or Google, where we are offered predictive phrases or items we might be interested in purchasing based on our browsing history, our brains and spirits offer back to us whatever we feed them. What we think about shows up in our lives over and over again, so finding ways to focus on positivity and life-giving ideas can impact our lives on so many levels.

It's one thing to say we need to focus on positive thoughts, but making that happen is something else entirely. This is especially true for people with trauma as our intrusive and negative thoughts can be so pervasive. We have learned that the very worst you can imagine— or had not even dared to imagine—can actually happen, and these experiences can create feelings of distrust and impending doom. It is important to make a plan, to live in gratitude and balance, and to be intentional in our thoughts.

As a person who has several allergies, I find that my approaches to both the way I eat and the way I think are very similar. I can't just head out on a trip without a plan for how to feed myself in a healthy way; if I have healthy food available when I am hungry, I can be sure to nourish my body rather than just filling it with something I may not be allergic to but is not as healthy. Similarly, if I don't have a plan for how to prevent or rid myself of negative thoughts—a plan for what I will feed my mind, my body, my spirit, and my emotions—then I will fall back into harmful thought patterns.

In moments when everything becomes too much, I have found it extremely beneficial to spend time creating in some way. For me, this may include drawing, writing, painting, or singing. Maybe for you this looks more like organizing, cooking, baking, or building. Sometimes, we put creativity into boxes; we think that unless we are painters, and a good painter at that, then we are not really creative. Personally, I believe that creativity comes in many shapes and forms. The important thing is leaving behind whatever is trying to take our attention, focussing that energy into something that can either be an interpretation of those feelings or can serve as a distraction from our thoughts and put our attention on something much healthier for us.

One example of this was a time when I had been struggling with anxiety and decided

Doing what I was born to do with the amazing talents of these gentlemen;
(left to right) Glenn Taylor, Gene Hardy, Vince Pollitt and Tim Murphy.
Photo credit: Dave Davies

to self-medicate with wine. I woke up in the morning hung over and filled with shame, not because I had done something horrible but because I didn't want to be relying on drinking to help me through my anxiety. I was ashamed because I was holding tightly to a set of rules that I thought would keep me safe—I was a worship leader in a church as well as working in ministry counselling others, and being drunk was not going to look good on my ministerial resume. And in truth, I was ashamed because I had been steeped in shame for most of my life, and I knew no way to escape.

That morning, I woke up and began praying, again. I asked God for forgiveness, again. I felt like an utter failure, again. I asked God, "Why do I do this? What is wrong with me?" And in response, I heard a soft, kind voice from somewhere within me that simply said, "Oh honey, it's okay. You just have issues. You all do."

For a moment, I was able to laugh at the situation and put away the critical way of thinking about myself. I cried and I laughed, and then I sat down and wrote a song called "I've Got Issues." Writing is a way for me to let go of whatever it is I am holding on to and embrace something new all at once. If I am afraid, I can write about that and also about what I might need to do to change those feelings. It is a release and an embrace all at once—a way to process my life in a way that is free to explore, unrestricted by thoughts of what should be. That morning, as I wrote that song, I went through every possible scenario I could think of around my issues and fears and phobias, and I had fun with it as well as facing it. This song will be coming out on a CD I will be releasing in 2022.

We truly are what we think, so finding ways to shift our thoughts from negative and accusatory to positive and encouraging is incredibly important to our mental health. Learning to speak to ourselves the way we would speak to a dear friend in any given situation is a good place to start. The process is not a quick one; it requires time, intention, and consistency. And when we fall, we get back up and start again.

Alison Perry-Davies
Photo credit: Lani Sanders

Photo credit: Lani Sanders

12

For God So Loved the World

"The spiritual journey is the unlearning of fear and the acceptance of love."
Marianne Williamson

Spirituality in its many forms can be beautiful, freeing, and healing. When we come from a place where we are unsure of what love, relationships, boundaries, and community might look like—or more importantly, what we want it to look like—it can be very attractive to find a community that believes in love and forgiveness. Sometimes, though, we may end up taking on someone else's beliefs as our own without truly weighing it all out.

As I have mentioned before, I have always been interested in spirituality and have explored many different aspects of it. Once, when I was about nine or so, my friend Suzie and I were playing in a fort we made in the forest by our house. We had hollowed out a bushy area that kept us hidden from the rest of the world, and we would sit in our magical fort, quiet as mice, and watch people walk by. I wanted more, though, so we went out and "borrowed" roses from gardens in the neighbourhood and lined the inside of the fort with these absolutely stunning flowers. I said it was our "church of the roses," and we began talking to the roses and, if my memory serves me correctly, even praying to them. This all came to an end when we told Suzie's dad about it—he was a wonderful man, and I am so grateful for his kindness in my life. However, as a Catholic, he wanted to teach us about what he believed in, and that was that we couldn't worship Jesus AND the flowers. When I look back on this memory today, I see two things: my desire to connect to something bigger than me as well as my longing to create and the joy that it gave me.

As I reached adulthood, I continued my search for something or someone that connected us all together. Like many people who are healing from trauma and trying to find some sense of meaning and hope, I longed for clear, black-and-white, right-and-wrong rules. I wanted to find something that would give me answers. I wanted to be loved and accepted and did not always understand how to find those things. I also lacked an understanding of and experience with true intimacy and boundaries.

One area I have found to be important to use discernment in, especially with a history of trauma and abuse, is the ideals and beliefs held by some of these organizations—things like modest dress codes for women (which might make a person feel they are being held responsible for lust in others), submission, and rules about what is okay to eat, drink, or listen to. There can be long lists of dos and don'ts controlling everyday life which I may or may not agree with. While I love spirituality and the wonderful community that churches can bring, I had to learn how to hold my own ideals and beliefs and not be swayed by well-meaning people who wanted to help but held opinions I did not necessarily share. This was not about them doing anything wrong; it was about me being unable, at those times, to discern for myself what I actually believed and being afraid to think for myself and take responsibility for my own beliefs. They didn't ask me to make them my conscience—that choice was born out of my own wounding and fear of doing things wrong. I needed to find my own faith, my own way, and if I really believed in a god or spirit or love force of any kind, then what was I so afraid of? How could I think that an all-loving being would not woo me and guide me as I fell and stumbled and searched and wondered?

I have come to a place where I see that it is not only okay but also completely reasonable to love Jesus or hold any spiritual belief AND believe in the possibilities of so many things we may not be able to see or touch or ever fully understand. The more I have learned, the more I realize that I really don't know much at all, so I stay open to and curious about everything around me. I don't need to have all the answers; in fact, it seems rather odd to me that anyone would. Instead, we hope and wonder and explore, and that is a beautiful place to be.

Very early on in my life, I learned that I did not get to choose who stayed and who left. All my tears and my begging would not make someone stay with me, call me, spend time with me, and ultimately, love me. I learned that I had no voice. I learned that people can touch you in ways you neither want nor understand, and that there is nothing I or anyone else can do about it. I learned that people with power get to say what happens to me, and I had no idea how to get that power over my own life. I learned that love, no matter how desperately I longed for it, would never really look or feel the same way it did in books or movies. Love was unkind and sometimes cruel. Love was a liar. Love was based on how hard I worked to please whoever it was that held it over me.

For those of us with trauma, a liar comes into our hearts and our minds and starts to spew venom at us, to us, about us. It reminds us we are not enough. It tells us that we cannot trust anyone. It lets us know that our choices are very limited, and that we need to do what we can to please the people in power if we want to survive.

As a result of all this, I was afraid to trust and often misinterpreted real kindness and real love as something alien. Healthy love felt so different that when I experienced it, I often thought something was wrong. Trauma twisted my intuitive knowings in a way that meant I could no longer trust myself and my own warning signals.

Eventually, my family and I were so blessed to find a beautiful church family where we found endless amounts of love and support and healing, and we spent over fifteen years in that community. It was here that I was first introduced to Elijah House Ministry and learned about how holding unforgiveness in my heart was really a poison to me—to any of us. I learned to explore the impact of trauma at a level that was connected to my faith, and I began to repair my relationship with God. Finally, I came to a place where I was able to ask myself, what if we allowed ourselves to wonder about the divine? What if we suspended all belief and disbelief, all previous teachings, all understanding and lack of understanding, and just wondered? What if we closed our eyes, sat quietly, and allowed all that is beautiful and kind and full of love to wash over us? What if we invited that in without any opinion or fear of what that might be?

What if we choose to begin or join or imagine or wonder about an absolute revolution of love? If we choose to participate with an energy force that only has intentions for us that are good, pure, and lovely? What if we suspend rules and regulations and religion and constraints for a moment and trust that if there is truly a god or creator or universe that has any love for

us, that this being or beings will love us beyond our fear and chaos?

For many years I have had visions of a blue, fluid-like mist that travels on notes through air and brings healing. There were times when I was leading worship in church and I would see this beautiful mist hover over and in and around an individual, almost like there was some sort of blockage being highlighted to me. In those moments, it seemed to me that I needed to pray and, mostly, to sing over and through whatever was impeding the flow. Much like someone would pray for healing, I would have this sense that there was a vibration of sorts that I was being invited to partner with, and that singing along with these musical vibrations of love would shift the blockage and allow healing to flow freely. I did not speak to others about this as I never knew exactly how to describe what was happening; I can only say that it felt spirit-led and natural, and that it came from a place of deep love. After studying a variety of sound and vibration therapies, I realized I had somehow intuitively been practicing these ancient methods.

Ultimately, as I moved along my path to healing, I began to see that love—healthy, true, real love—was much different than what I had been experiencing, receiving, or offering. Instead, love is just as it is spoken about in 1 Corinthians 13: 4-9. I have interpreted these verses as they apply to my own life, and I'd like to share that interpretation here.

For many years I have had visions of a blue, fluid-like mist that travels on notes through air and brings healing.

Waves of Blue by Alison Perry-Davies

This was a wonderfully healing process for me to paint and was so close to how I experience the blue mist when I sing over people. To create this multimedia piece I first chose items to attach to the canvas and then I painted it, layer after layer and in between I took it to the shower and used the shower head to bleed the colours. This was a beautifully somatic process for me.

99

4   Love works best when we wait for each other, and when we don't try to squish people into our ideas of how they should look or feel or act. Love is kind. Love doesn't try to control or turn things into a competition; rather, it celebrates with us when we succeed and stands right beside us in our challenges and failures. Love is a great cheerleader!

5   Love covers us. Love has our back. Love is proud of us and brags about us and thinks and says wonderful things to and about us, whether we are there or not. Love calms itself before it speaks to us if we are having a rough time, and if we screw up, love doesn't keep throwing that in our face. Love lets go of the resentment and does whatever it can to help us keep going forward.

6   Love isn't happy to see things go wrong or to see someone mess up. Love doesn't laugh and say "oh, I saw that coming" to or about anyone. Love is so compassionate and takes up so much space that pettiness and jealousy and judgements can't squeeze in beside it. We need to choose which one we give space to, and choosing love is always a good choice.

7   Love always protects, always trusts, always hopes, always perseveres. Love never gives up on us. No matter how bad things get, love sticks around and helps pick up the pieces.

8   Love covers us and protects us. It stands guard and watches over us. Love doesn't look for what is wrong with us. Instead, love looks for what is wonderful about us and nurtures those things. Love sees embers barely glowing and fans them back to a flame. Love doesn't quit on us. Love is loyal and true.

9   Love never fails because it won't give up. Love says, "No matter what, I am here with you, and I'm not going anywhere. We can fix this, together."

True, real love comes to our side, stands with us in the midst of all the carnage, and doesn't look away. Love always looks for ways to overtake us and free us of all that holds us back. Whatever the question is, love is always the answer.

Sometimes we find love in a church, in a kind word spoken by a friend, or in being able to finally tell a dark secret. Sometimes, love is in the eyes of a person willing to forgive us when we have messed up beyond what we thought was possible. Maybe love comes to you as a god or a spiritual practice or a beautiful relationship. Maybe love comes layer by layer, moving in through cracks created by counselling or various healing modalities.

The most beautiful love is, of course, self-love, though it is not always an easy one to embrace. I know many people say that if we don't love ourselves then we cannot love anyone else or receive love, but I am not sure that I would agree with that statement—not as an absolute, at least. I can say without a doubt that many wonderful people loved me before I really knew how to love myself, and that I received that love to the best of my ability. I can also say with absolute certainty that although I struggled to love myself, I adored my children, always. Today, though, I am better able to share with them a healthy love, a less selfish form of love, a more giving and kind love.

The Bible tells us that God is love, as do many of the great religions. A beautiful Tamil

---

True, real love comes to our side, stands with us in the midst of all the carnage, and doesn't look away. Love always looks for ways to overtake us and free us of all that holds us back. Whatever the question is, love is always the answer.

---

hymn named Kandha Guru Kavasam quotes, "Oh holy Great flame, Grant me with love. You said the spreading love is Para Brahma / For the thing which is everywhere is only Love / And Love is the only thing which is like a soul within us / Love is Kumara, Love is Kandha." This idea resonates with me. I have been exploring and challenging my own beliefs, and I am no longer satisfied or at peace with imagining that I or any of us has all the answers and somehow knows "THE" truth, if that even exists. Instead, I am coming to see more and more clearly that when we practice love, we are participating with creation and the creator and a wonderfully mysterious energy that I have come to believe is really beyond our comprehension. I no longer feel a need to define this mystical presence—to label or control what or how others may experience this. I simply believe that love itself is a beautiful, powerful force that has the capacity to heal in ways I could not have imagined. Finding a relationship with love brought me to a place where I finally felt like I was home.

Your Love

BY ALISON PERRY-DAVIES

Your Love
Gives me hope for tomorrow
Your Love Tastes much sweeter than wine
Your Love
Lifts me out of the darkness
Chases fears away
That are no longer mine.

Many waters can not quench Love
Many rivers can not wash it away.

Your Love
Is the rock that I cling to
Your Love Breathes peace to my pain
Your Love Is beyond understanding
Speaks truth into lies
I am forever changed.

13

ForgiveMess

"To forgive is to set a prisoner free and discover that the prisoner was you."
Lewis B. Smedes

Forgiveness is a word that gets thrown around in everything from self-help books to spiritual retreats. For me, I found out that forgiveness isn't so much about writing straight on crooked lines as it is finding a way to dance on the path we were given, whatever those lines may be.

I think our responses can show so much about where we are at and how we are processing information. And for me, forgiveness was not my natural response to pain or betrayal. It was not what I wanted to hear or read about when I was looking for ways to get beyond the depth of my hopelessness. I wanted justice. I wanted wrongs to be righted, people to pay for their "sins." As I slowly began healing from the trauma I had experienced, I began to see that forgiveness is the path that leads us out of this web-like jungle of despair.

It took a long time, but I finally came to a place where I could understand that forgiveness is messy. There are so many layers of forgiveness, to the point that I have come to know it as forgive*mess*. The whole process can be messy and confusing. Why do I forgive? When do I forgive? What do I forgive? Have I counted the cost? Do I *need* to forgive?

After my daughter was raped, I was consumed by hate and anger. For many years, I lived in a state of anxiety that made it difficult for me to hold a thought. At one time I was prepared to have the person who did this horrible, unthinkable thing to my daughter be maimed in such a way that he would have welcomed death, but I did not want that wish granted. It was not until I had experienced the dream in which I saw the man receive an absolute understanding of the suffer ing he had caused, along with some deep counselling, that I was able to rid myself of this desire for revenge and all the negativity and rage that came with it.

I didn't come to forgiveness by way of a single apology or prayer or counselling session. Instead, it was a long road I walked that had potholes and twists. It came with moaning and wailing and grief. It came through searching and hoping and desperation. It came when I tried absolutely everything else because I didn't want to let go of the hate I held on to until I could see that the grip I had on my bitterness was actually choking the life from me. It came when I saw there was no other choice, and then a lifetime of regret poured over me in a series of moments. It was harsh and painful and messy, so very messy, and then—and only then— was I free.

---

*It took a long time, but I finally came to a place
where I could understand that forgiveness is messy.
There are so many layers of forgiveness,
to the point that I have come to know it as
ForgiveMess.*

Forgiveness was not in the words I spoke to someone in a single moment, nor was it in the prayer that would bring me sudden relief or the pressure I felt to let things go.

Forgiveness first came in moments where I thought it was what I "should" do. I scratched and fought to loosen the claws that unforgiveness and resentment and hate had dug into my very soul. I knew I needed to find forgiveness because without it, I was nothing but a container of agony and hate and fear. I had come to a place where the world and everyone in it were a threat, an enemy, a constant reminder that I would never be the person I pretended to be, never be safe, never be free. I fought for and against forgiveness until one day, there it was.

Forgiveness came in layers, in moments, piece by piece. I found forgiveness through the dream I had where I saw the torment of the man who raped my daughter. I found forgiveness through reading *The Shack*, with all the stops and starts and wrestling with my own pain and fear before finally letting myself begin to see that there could be hope after a dark night of the soul. I found forgiveness when I went to counselling, and when I prayed, and when I began to see us all as beings finding our way through the challenges of life. I found forgiveness as I peeled back the layers of blame I had carefully placed on others and started to witness the pain and shame they experience. I found forgiveness when I finally stopped seeing myself in the role of victim and began to climb out from the rubble. I found forgiveness for others as I realized the pain I had caused to so many around me. I found forgiveness when I witnessed aching regret in the eyes of those who had brought me suffering.

One of the most difficult parts of this process was removing the judgements I had placed on myself. I had to align the person I wanted to be with the deep down, raw and honest, no-more-bullshit person that I am, with all of my flaws and knee-jerk reactions and thoughts and fears and pain and dreams and hopes. THAT forgiveness, self-forgiveness, was the one that eluded me the longest.

Sometimes learning to just let go is one of the sweetest gifts of all. The other day I was driving somewhere in my convertible, top down and windows up, and found myself rehashing a recent conversation in my head. Someone had said something that irritated me, and I had replied with something I probably shouldn't have. I was allowing this brief moment of tension to occupy much more space than it required or deserved. Then, as I came to stop at a red light, a feeling came over me. I became aware of something so gentle and lovely and smooth—like warm, freshly-made pudding. I felt a softness all around me, like velour or satin. I was literally breathing in peace and love and comfort; I could not hold the thoughts I'd been mulling over and have this experience at the same time.

And then, there it was: a beautiful white and pale-yellow butterfly. It was as if it floated into my car and heart and spirit all at once. It gently flitted around me, fluttering and floating, and somewhere within me I heard, *Let it go honey, let it go.* It was so calming and peaceful, and I was completely enveloped in a bubble of love. I can't say I know for sure what happened or how, but I *can* tell you my heart felt visited, and that I am so grateful for whimsical, mystical visits like this one.

Holding on to negative feelings and conversations in our thoughts—whether they are about past hurts, ways we may have been wronged, feelings that life has been unfair, or mistakes we have made—gives those things power over us. Finding ways to forgive and let go of all that holds us back opens us up to more control and healing, ultimately leading us to balanced, peaceful, joyful lives

14

Piece by Shattered Piece

"The wound is the place where the light enters you."
Rumi

A beautiful vase slowly grows one crack, then two. Lines spread across the glass as it becomes worn and tattered and bumped. And then one day, it shatters and pieces scatter far and wide. They hide under counters and behind furniture and in corners you can't imagine they could have reached.

After the panic settles, we see we are trapped in a shattered web of glass waiting to harm us with any move we might make. We survey our surroundings, assessing the damage. Okay, it doesn't look too bad. We can see where the pieces are, and some came off in big chunks. Big chunks are always good because they are easier to find, easier to place back in their rightful spot—or what is left of the spot they came from.

As we slowly pick up the obvious pieces, we must be careful, oh so careful. That smooth lovely vase now has ragged edges that can cut us, as we have learned through experience. We go slower now; we know the pain of retrieval. We know the cost. We know we must respect the jagged pieces and their ability to wound us deeply.

It appears the floor around us is cleared, yet there are tiny pieces, almost invisible to the naked eye, that can easily cut or imbed themselves in our skin. And so goes the search, carefully looking for each piece, wondering where it might fit into the shattered vase.

This is a spirit broken.

When we experience trauma, we become shattered, and recovering the pieces has its own risks. And just like the vase, our mind, our spirit, is never going to look quite the same. No matter how well we are able to glue things back together, some of the cracks will show and some pieces may never be found. We carefully gather what we can, and we will fill in the gaps with what we can find—sometimes just to hold things together, sometimes because what we have found to fill in the hole is beautiful to our eyes and to the eyes of another.

Our lives are much like a kintsukuroi pottery bowl. Kintsukuroi, or kintsugi, is the traditional Japanese art of repairing a bowl or vase with lacquer and gold, highlighting the seam where the cracks once were. The technique joins fragments, blending what was damaged with what is new, refining the piece with the understanding that it is more beautiful for having been broken.

Embracing our brokenness and loving ourselves back to wholeness creates a new heart—a kintsukuroi heart. Some of the most amazing people I have ever known are people who have been shattered and were willing to do whatever it took to heal and create their own beautiful heart laced with gold.

Just as it takes fire to make gold pure, healing from trauma is not as simple as just gluing ourselves back together. Sometimes, a piece doesn't join right and falls off; sometimes, the whole vase falls apart, and we have to start over. The process is ongoing, repairing and replacing piece by piece as many times as it takes. It can be a lifetime of learning. In those moments when things break once again, we can be less than we hoped for—not necessarily rising to the occasion, acting with less than grace or kindness to ourselves and others. Yet a quick trip to the dark side, as it were, is not a sign that all is lost and we were never healed. Rather, it is a reminder to check that we are doing what we need to do to give ourselves the best chance living life in peace and wholeness.

Sometimes, that inner accuser would try to convince me that one moment is who I truly am. But no one moment defines any of us, ever. A moment, no matter how wonderful or horrible, is just that: a moment.

*Embracing our brokenness and loving
ourselves back to wholeness creates a new heart
—a kintsukuroi heart.
Some of the most amazing people
I have ever known are people who have been
shattered and were willing to do
whatever it took to heal and create their own
beautiful heart laced with gold.*

On this journey of healing from trauma, there is no finish line we cross. We are always looking for strategies to bring relief, peace, and healing. We are continuously putting the pieces of ourselves back together to create a new whole. We are learning more and more about ourselves, about how to bring together who we are and who we want to be. And little by little, layer by layer, freedom comes.

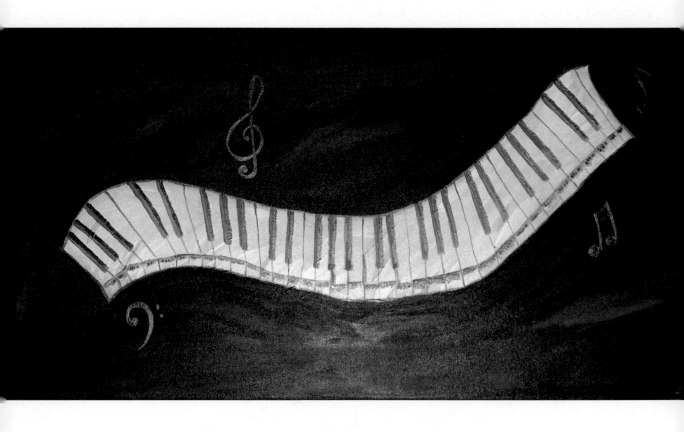

Burning Desire by Alison Perry-Davies

"Burning Desire" poured out of my longing to play piano after my brain injury.

Part 3

Visions, Whispers, and Knowings

15

A Thin Line

"Ode sees things that I cannot see. Maybe he's just a little bit closer to God than me and there's a line between what's real and what is not, and it's a thin line."
Mark Perry, *"Ode"*

The line above is from one of my all-time favourite songs, written by my cousin Mark Perry. He is an amazing storyteller, and there is something so beautiful and healing about his music. The first time I listened to one of his songs, I realized that the buzzing I usually heard in my head when music was being played was not present. I can only guess that the gentleness of his music and voice was soothing enough for me to be able to listen to it, and that enough healing had occurred that I was ready. Slowly I was able to listen to more and more of his songs, and eventually I was able to listen to other music as well. This was another time where art brought me healing, and I cannot fully express the gratitude I feel toward him or the connection I feel to his music now.

I have this feeling, a small inkling in me, that somehow his music delivered to me a healing balm from our ancestors. I can't explain why it feels like that, only that it does. Sometimes I think that this feeling or connection was sent by Nana Perry, Dad's mum, whom

113

I never met as she passed before I was born. I've heard that she was quite a wonderful woman, and when I became a nana myself, I remember thinking about all the love she would have had for me. In Indigenous and Celtic cultures, it is believed that our ancestors are not just part of how we came to be; we also carry them and their stories as part of us. Somehow, there seemed an impartation Mark had connected to that I had not—at least, not yet.

"We do not become storytellers.

We came as carriers of the stories

we and our ancestors actually lived. We are.

Some of us are still catching up to what we are."

— **Dr. Clarissa Pinkola Estes**

While I adore all of Mark's music, this particular line speaks to me. When I think of the thin line between what is real and what is not, I think of the whispers we sometimes hear from the invisible realm—those deep knowings, revelatory visions, or intuitions that resonate somewhere deep within us. That warm, gentle wind that leads to a truth so sweet that it changes us. That place. That voice. That invitation for us to follow.

There have been times when I was not able to trust those inner knowings as a result of trauma-induced insecurities and a long list of poor choices. I spent many years listening, studying, praying, and meditating in an effort to understand the difference between my wounding and the nudge of spirit. Eventually, I was able to come to a place where I trust myself and am trusted by the people around me.

For some time, I led a prophetic group in the church community we were part of—a group of people who longed to have creation and the creator speak to them. As part of this, I was asked to create a course for those interested in exploring the Prophetic, as we called it in church, though it may also be called psychic or intuitive or revelatory. This course was for those interested in learning to listen to and trust that inner voice, and to differentiate between what was real and what was not.

One of the most important things I have learned to watch for is quite simple: the voice that leads us to understanding—whether we believe that to be our own inner voice or the universe, God, whatever that may be for us—brings calm. That voice speaks of love. That voice never feels rushed or anxious or overwhelming in a way that has us worried. It brings calm, and it always leads to love.

As a child, I would often have knowings and dreams; sometimes I tried to share them, but mostly I kept them locked inside. But when I was eleven, a moment came that taught me to trust these intuitions. Our nana, who lived with us, became quite ill and had to be rushed to the hospital. As my brother Bruce and his friend were carrying her down the hall, I was desperate to say goodbye to her. Somewhere deep down, I knew I would never see her again.

I tried to get out of my bedroom and into the hall where Nana was being carried out, but the door was being held shut. Someone called out, "Not now, Nana is sick!" I kept pounding on the door; I was relentless. Today, I understand that she was frail and frightened, and that two teenaged boys were doing their best to carry her down the hall, down the stairs, and out to the vehicle to rush her to the hospital. They had too much to deal with already. At the time, though, I was devastated. I just knew I was never going to see her again. I had not experienced death before, but something in me knew she was going to die, and I had to say goodbye. I called to her out my bedroom window, and dear Nana tried to be so brave and waved to me.

On Sunday, about a week after Nana went into the hospital, we were all getting dressed up to go visit her when Dr. Olson pulled into the driveway. I saw Mum's face, and I knew that she knew something was wrong. They went into another room to talk. A little while later, Mum came out with the doctor, and he told us that Nana had passed away in her sleep.

I cried myself to sleep that night. I knew she was going to die, and now she was gone. My fear of not seeing her again was now a reality. Oh, but in my dreams that night, Nana came to me. I saw her, as clear as could be, and she told me not to worry and said goodbye. When I woke up, I felt so comforted that I was able to see her one last time and to have that closure.

Over the next little while, I wrote one of my first songs. I waited a few days to share it with Mum as she wasn't doing very well; she was on her own with five kids, and now her absolute rock was gone.

I remember knocking on Nana's bedroom door—well, it was Mum's bedroom now. Mum called to me in a soft, shaky tone, inviting me to come in. I sat down on Nana's brown couch and told Mum I had written a song to make her feel better. I asked if I could sing it for her. "Of course, sweetie," she replied, and so I sang it. I still remember it, too.

Gone

Gone, no more shall she come

Gone, away from us all

He drove up today

Early in the morning

We all cried

Cause she had died

Can you even imagine? My poor mumma. She smiled and told me the song was lovely, and then said she needed to rest for a little while.

I don't think Bob Dylan or Leonard Cohen felt the earth tremble with these lyrics. However, this was the very first time that I learned how healing art and creativity could be—I felt a sense of calm and a release as I wrote them. I also learned to trust those little knowings that would come to me from time to time for the rest of my life.

Gentle whispers, small voices, little knowings, gut reactions, intuition—these are some of the many terms used to describe when there is a connection, sense, or feeling that guides us. I have spoken with family, friends, and clients who have struggled with mental health issues where delusions and voices were a part of their experience, and that is not what I am talking about here. Those voices do not bring peace or guidance or clarity, but rather anxiety. Instead of community and togetherness, they create isolation. I have not ever personally experienced those intrusive voices in my mind and my life, but those who have explained them to me describe a very different experience than the gentle, loving inner knowing I am talking about.

For me, learning to live my life on a more integrative and holistic path includes seeing myself and my life in a way that includes all parts as one rather than dissecting the mental from the physical, the emotional, or the spiritual. I think it is important for us to listen to the voice inside us that seems to know us so well and have our best interest at heart. The voice that calms us. The voice that brings us through and helps us decide what choice to make.

There have been times in my healing journey when I have felt so close to the creator that I could almost feel a breath on my face. In these times, there was always a voice, a knowing that was calling me, guiding me, loving me, healing me, comforting me, and reminding me of all I was created for. And in those moments, I truly felt like I was coming home.

16

Counselling, Intuition, and Layers of Understanding

"Listen in silence because if your heart is full of other things,
you cannot hear the voice of God."

Sister Teresa

One Friday afternoon, I received a last-minute call from a friend. He let me know that he was helping run a week-long retreat which started on Monday, and they were short a prayer counsellor. Would I be available to help? I agreed, feeling both nervous and excited about what the week might hold.

Each day at this retreat, there would be teachings in the morning and in the afternoon. After each of these sessions, the participants would receive counselling and/or prayer and be able to work on some of what they felt stirring during the teachings. The participants signed up with a counsellor at the start of the week, two per counsellor, and that is who they would work with every day.

When I checked who had signed up with me, I was troubled to see that one of them was a man. Although I had done quite a bit of healing around my own sexual trauma as well as my daughter's, I still found myself feeling uneasy about being alone in a room with a man

I didn't know. I spoke with my friend who was running the retreat about my nervousness, and he offered to change things around for me. I responded that I would do it, I just wanted him to know that I felt nervous because I was concerned that my insecurities might lessen the experience for this person. My friend and I chatted for a bit, and after that I felt confident enough to move forward.

On the first day, I opened myself to hearing whatever might be helpful for the people I would be working with. As I did this, information that I had no way of knowing started to come to me. I have no great explanation for how this works, other than that I believe there is an energetic force that connects us all on a deeper level. I had knowledge come to me about both individuals I would be counselling, and some of it was quite personal. In particular, I had a very strong sense about the man that I needed to really ponder, to pray on, in order to be certain about it. This was not something that I could just say without really being clear, especially because what came to me could have been from my own fear or wounding. In fact, I suspected that this was the case, and I was actually doubting myself and my capabilities. It was so detailed and would be so very wrong to say if it wasn't true. If.

As the days went by, this quiet knowing began to weigh on my heart. Despite that, the man and I had great sessions every day, and we were all growing and healing, as is the way these things go. On the last day, though, the weight of the message was becoming almost unbearable. The man and I were doing our last session, and there was maybe half an hour left before the participants headed home—my window to say something was closing. My heart was pounding in my chest. My hands were sweating. My own voice was so loud in my head that I could barely think. It was saying to me, *You can't. You cannot say this thing! If you are wrong, if this is just you being messed up because of your own abuse, then this is going to be so damaging.*

And yet somewhere deep inside, I knew I had to speak up. I could not let this moment pass. I started out suddenly, becoming awkward with my conversation. I told the man that I felt I needed to share a bit about my own story (which is not something we would typically do) and then told him about the sexual abuse I experienced as a child. I could feel that this wasn't what I needed to share; it just didn't land right inside of me. Then I told him about my daughter—about her rape, about court, about the mark that it all left on me as a mother who had trusted someone and allowed them access to my precious little girl.

I was so focussed on sharing this story that I was unaware of my surroundings. When

118

I finished, I looked at his face and realized he was sobbing. He then shared with me what he had done. He had been married to a woman who had a daughter, and as that daughter had aged and developed, he had allowed himself to watch her and think of her in ways he should not have. He then went on to act on those fantasies and sexually abused her for some time. Eventually he became a Christian and was completely changed, so he went to the police and turned himself in without a word to anyone. He was charged and served time in prison, which he had finished many years ago.

I didn't know what to think or do at first. My mind was spinning. Here I was, sitting with a man, sharing with him, caring for him all week, and he was a man like the one who had destroyed me, my daughter, our lives, and our family. And then something happened that I will never forget: the bitterness I had felt for years was replaced with compassion.

I looked at the man and told him that he was not created for this, and that what he did and who he was were not the same. I told him that as the mother of a daughter who had been raped, I wanted to speak forgiveness over him. He responded that he had done what he could to make amends to the girl he had abused and asked her forgiveness, and she had given it to him. However, he had asked his ex-wife to forgive him as well, and she had told him she never would. And so, his heart's desire was to receive forgiveness from a mother of a daughter who had been sexually abused.

I can't even imagine what the statistical chances are for a mother of a sexually abused daughter to be the person who did this particular healing method with this particular man. All I can say is that it brought about an enormous amount of healing for both of us. He was able to find healing through being offered forgiveness, and I found healing in being able to see an abuser as a person first—a person who did something unthinkable, yes, and who lived with that shame and regret. I knew in those moments that he was so much more than his past.

To be clear, forgiveness is not about wiping the slate clean to the point of becoming foolish or unwise. I'm not saying that this person should have access to children, for example. Instead, it removes that huge hook in our side that pulls and rips and tears at us, tethering us to the other person by a heavy chain.

For me, it allowed me to see a person that I once would have had nothing but hate for with new eyes. I had lived life as a slave to my pain and bitterness, and this experience brought me relief, healing, and freedom. Please know that I understand how rare this experience was, and that these words could be a trigger for many. My path has not been one that many would

likely choose, although I would say that my path chose me more that I chose it. What I am trying to share is that there can be a way to untangle ourselves from a person or an event that has held us captive and caused us so much torment.

After this experience, I went on to work in correctional facilities as a disability case manager and worked with men who were incarcerated for a variety of offences, including sexual offences. I also worked for years counselling and ministering to men who lived with deep shame and struggled with so many issues around their sexuality and the abuse they had perpetrated. The same woman who once imagined having damage done to the person who harmed my daughter was now sitting across the table from offenders and having compassion for them. Part of my job was to find resources for those who wanted to change, helping them find ways to heal from their own traumas—many of them had been victims of abuse themselves. I did not become careless, but rather mindful and open to possibilities. As a person who spent decades living in the aftermath of trauma, I knew too well not only the abuses I had experienced but also the abuses I was capable of inflicting on others. My heart had been changed, and through that I reached a powerful place to live my life from.

Blue Mist Mountain by Alison Perry-Davies

"Blue Mist Mountain" was created playing with textures using only a pallet knife. It was a very calming experience.

17

Trusting the Still, Small Voice

"The value of taking risks through all stages of life is constant…
it's the excuses that change."
Rik Leaf, *Four Homeless Millionaires*

I t started with a dream, as many of my stories seem to, although I supposed it truly started a little further back than that.

I have loved Mavis Staples since I was a little girl. I adored how she not only sang about love, compassion, and equality but also seemed to live it with such grace. Every time The Staples Singers would come on the radio, my heart would race. I would grab my brush, look into my mirror, and sing along with Mavis with everything I could conjure up inside of me. With all that was happening in the world at large, and within my own little world, Mavis really did take me somewhere else.

Fast forward to 2006, and one morning I woke up from a dream—the kind of a dream that makes you want to go back to sleep so you can be there again. In my dream, I met Mavis Staples. She and I talked and laughed, and she passed her mantle to me. Me! Mavis Staples passed her mantle to me! For those who haven't heard this term—I've learned that not everyone has—it is used to describe a person who holds some sort of authority gifting and passing a portion of that along to another person.

Part of my healing journey has been walking into all I have been called to do and sharing that in a way that might encourage and inspire others to do the same. Mavis had done this for me my entire life, and I wanted to do what she has been doing so beautifully for all these decades: choosing to share spirit and love without apology or pretence or preaching.

Mavis Staples has walked in that love through the civil rights movement—through times when people must have treated her so horribly based on her gender and the colour of her skin. Yet despite this unkindness, she has had a career and life where she has shone as a beacon of light and love regardless of race, religion, social standing, or any other way we might divide ourselves. She figured this out so long ago in my eyes, and she is an incredible example of what it looks like to live life through the lens of love, forgiveness, and creativity.

After receiving this dream, I believed that I was going to meet Mavis, that we would connect, and that there might be some transference or blessing. I didn't really understand how any of this would occur. I just knew in my heart that this chubby little redhead from Victoria, BC, was somehow going to be meeting with this Grammy award-winning Rock and Roll Hall of Famer, and that it was going to be fabulous.

In April of 2006, opportunity arose. Mavis Staples and Taj Mahal were going to be playing in Victoria, and I bought my tickets. I was so excited. I mean, obviously this was when we would meet, right? What could go wrong?

I showed up early and hung around outside for a while, then in the lobby once it opened. I wanted to give Miss Mavis Staples every opportunity to see me and call me over, but it didn't happen. The show started, and she was, of course, brilliant. As she was leaving, she said she loved us all, and then she looked at a few people and said it directly to them—myself included. I was so happy to be in her presence and to have her speak directly to me, but it didn't seem like my dream. I went home floating on her performance and yet disappointed that I had gotten it so wrong.

A few months later, Dave was watching TV and called me into the room. He showed me an advertisement declaring that Mavis would be coming back to Vancouver Island to play at the Island Music Fest. "This is it!" he said. "You have to go!" I asked him to come with me, but he told me that it was my thing—something I needed to do.

That Friday, I was preparing to head out to the beautiful Comox Valley, where the festival was being held, when the phone rang. It was my friend Skye, and she was having a difficult time. One of those knowings came into my mind and told me I needed to invite her. Truth be told, I struggled with this idea for a minute; this was my opportunity to meet Mavis, after all. However, I knew I needed to invite her, so I told her exactly what was going on: the dream, the festival, and my intention to speak with Mavis Staples. I told her that she could come and tell me what's going on, but we needed to go to Comox together. She agreed, and off we went.

After a three-and-a-half-hour drive, during which we had a long talk about her life, we met up with a friend we were going to be staying with that night and then headed out to the festival. Soon we arrived at the fairground, which was a beautiful open field with the smell of food vendors wafting through the air and a sea of smiling faces sparkling in the sun. We found ourselves a place to sit, and then it was time to sort out what happened next. I was here; now what?

The grounds were set up for the show, and I decided to just take my shot. Skye and I headed over to a stage at the far end of the field. The backstage area was fenced off, with a couple of gates for entry and lots of security hanging around. I could see fifth wheel trailers, food trucks, sitting areas, and other such things set up for the entertainers. Suddenly, things were getting very real.

I rather nervously went to the gate and asked if I could speak to someone who might be in charge of setting up meetings with Mavis Staples. I wasn't sure how this was going to go. After all, how do you explain that you've had a dream, and now you believe you're supposed to come and see this famous singer? That's a hard sell for anybody.

Soon a woman arrived who they said was in charge. I said that I had a message for Miss Staples, and would there be any way that I could meet with her? It seemed to be going okay so far—this woman was actually talking to me, at least, so we were off to a good start. Then Skye leans across and says, "Yeah, she's had like a vision from God or something."

Oh my God, I think to myself, *don't say that. She'll think I'm a lunatic.* I say rather awkwardly, "Well, I just, you know, I just have a message that I need to give to her."

To my surprise, the woman said, "Well, sure you can, but she's not here yet. Later on, after the show, you'll be able to talk to her." I was dizzy with excitement; my dream was going to come true!

We went back to enjoy the festival. Mavis Staples came out and was brilliant as always, but then she was gone. I went back to the gate, and the woman we had chatted with earlier was nowhere to be seen. It seemed that I wasn't going to get to meet Mavis after all. I had so clearly felt in my heart that today was going to be the day I received her mantle, but now the show was over and nothing had happened. I was just standing in the field, watching the clock and wondering how I could have been so wrong.

Skye told me she needed to use the washroom, and I said I would stay where I was and wait for her. So I waited, and I waited, and I waited. After about twenty minutes I was starting to get a bit concerned, but then I looked toward the backstage area and see this very beautiful, very large black man heading my way. I immediately know who it is: the bass player for Mavis Staples. He walks right up to me and says, "Miss Alison?" My jaw dropped; how did this guy know who I am? He continued, "Miss Mavis will see you now." He then put his arm out so that we could link arms, as a Southern gentleman does. I hesitated, worried that my friend would come back from the washroom and I wouldn't be there, but this was my chance and I couldn't miss it. I took his arm, and he escorted me toward Mavis' dressing room.

We arrived backstage and there was a lot going on. Instruments were flying back and forth, and people were everywhere. As we walk through the area, I see Skye standing with a man who I later learned was the head of security. I was in shock. How did she get there?

Later, Skye explained to me that she had gone to the washroom, and then she went up to some security guards she saw standing around. She asked who the head of security was, and once he identified himself, she told him, "Look, my friend, I know you don't know her, but I do. She had a dream that she is supposed to talk to Mavis Staples, and my friend doesn't just say things like that. If she says that happened, then it really happened. I don't need to go see Miss Staples, I'm not trying to go meet her for myself. It's just for my friend." In response, the head of security looked at her and said, "Is she here to receive her mantle?"

I was astounded when I heard this. I hadn't told anyone about that part of my dream, not even my friend. I wasn't even sure how I was going to say that to Mavis Staples.

Skye said she replied, "Well, I don't even know what that is. I just know that if my friend said she is supposed to talk to her, then she is supposed to talk to her." And so the head of security made it happen.

My mind was racing as we approached Mavis' trailer, then knocked on the door. Mavis' sister Yvonne answered, and she was even more beautiful in person. I try to find words and fumble out something like, "I'm here. I've got… I have a message for Miss Mavis Staples." And

Miss Yvonne so gently said, "You know, her voice is not doing well right now. Could you come back tomorrow?"

My heart dropped. I explained that I couldn't come back as I had to head back to Victoria to attend a wedding. And then I heard from the back of the trailer, "A wedding? Oh, I do love me a wedding." And around the corner walked Miss Mavis Staples. Her eyes were so warm and so kind, and she invited me in. I was now standing in the trailer with Mavis and Yvonne Staples, along with my friend Skye and the head of security.

My mind raced. My first thought was, *She's so short*, followed quickly by, *I can't believe I'm standing here*. I took a long slow breath to calm myself, and then I looked right into her beautiful face and said, "Miss Staples, I understand that you are just a person, but you see, you are a very important person to me. I am so very grateful that I am getting this opportunity to speak with you. Right now, I am just trying to calm myself so that I can actually say what I came here to say."

Mavis was incredibly kind and gracious. She gently touched my arm and said, "Oh honey, that's just like when I met Lena Horne. I loved her my whole life, and then the moment I got to meet her, I just stood there all silly. I couldn't say a word, not a word I tell you. Now, you just take your time. And you remember, it's just me. This is just me, Mavis. You just take your time and tell me what you came to tell me."

And so I did. I told her all about my dream, and while she didn't really understand what I meant by the mantle part at first, she gave me space to talk until we both were clear on what I was trying to say. Then I told her, "You know, people talk about crossover music as if it's some new thing, but you've been doing it since the sixties. You've been crossing spiritual music and mainstream music your whole career, like almost fifty years. You have been bringing the spirit with you and sharing that love everywhere you go. It has never mattered where you were or who you were singing to, the love you carried shone bright."

Well, Mavis lit up with a smile so wide, and she said, "That's right! Yvonne, Yvonne. That's just what…" She started to get teary. "That's what I've been saying. Yvonne, listen to this, it is exactly what I've been talking about. We've been doing this for years, and they're all talking like it's something new."

"No, it's nothing new," I responded. "You crossed those boundaries a long time ago, and there was no looking back. You brought this beautiful message of love and spirituality, and you've been doing that for fifty years." Mavis hugged me, and we laughed with tears in our eyes. It was so meaningful for me to give that message to her; she had been using creativity to share love, hope, joy, and healing for all these years, and I wanted to make sure she knew the impact she had on so many people, myself included. I knew that carrying the weight and presence of that kind of grace and love likely came with its fair share of costs over the years.

We talked about so many beautiful things. We talked about my life and how I travelled around in search of this moment with her. She shared some stories about being on the road with Dr. Martin Luther King Junior, life with Pops Staples and the band, and the early days of the civil rights movement. Then she said to me, "I think I know what you mean about this mantle. Basically, you just want some of what I got.

"Yes," I said, "that's basically what it is. There's a thing that you walk in that is very powerful and beautiful and sacred, and I'm just asking if you would consider imparting some of that anointing to me, and if maybe we could just pray together."

She said, "Alison from Victoria, I will be happy and honoured to do that, but I want to tell you one thing: you don't need anything from me. You already have it. You light up a room when you walk into it."

She then looked at my friend Skye, who said, "That is exactly right, Miss Mavis. You should hear her sing."

I was overwhelmed. Mavis was more than a celebrity to me; she was a person who had molded a lot about how I saw the world. She had shaped how I sang and saw music and what I wanted to do. It felt as though she'd been mentoring me my whole life, even though I'd never met her before now. She taught me that love is a verb, a way of being, a way of speaking and sharing. She taught me that who we are singing to and where we are singing does not change that message. So, to hear her say that I did not need anything from her because I already had it touched me deeply. It seemed that this was part of an impartation of her mantle: her energy, the love that she so consistently walked in and shared from for so many years.

Mavis said she would pray with me, so we all stood in a circle and held hands—Yvonne, Mavis, me, Skye, and the head of security, whose name was Brian. I thanked God for all of them and for Pop Staples who'd had the vision for The Staples Singers, had mentored those girls, and had never given up. Mavis was so excited I had included him in the prayer; she loved her dad so much. At this point we had spent over an hour together, and Mavis said that while she could have talked longer, her driver needed to get back to his family. She finished with, "I'm going to say goodbye for now, Alison from Victoria. It's been a joy to meet you."

This experience was very powerful for me, and it was something that changed me very much.

One of the lessons that I was reminded of that day was to listen to that still, small voice within me. I had a dream, and in that dream something very beautiful and powerful happened. I followed it and didn't give up on it, and then there I was, getting to meet and actually spend time with this person who had so deeply impacted my life from afar. I am grateful that moments like these are part of what has shaped me and healed me.

At times, trauma has prevented me from trusting my inner knowings. Through experiences like this one, I have learned to really trust others, and more importantly, to trust *myself*.

Illustration by Mary Engelbreit

"She Illuminates" a gift from Francis Dick.
A painting of me singing with the raven in the background.

18

Time Is an Illusion

"Spirituality is a brave search for the truth about existence,
fearlessly peering into the mysterious nature of life."
Elizabeth Lesser

My healing journey has included moments when I have been given glimpses into the realm where the visible and the invisible collide. It is a kaleidoscope of beauty and colour and hope, always hope. One such experience came from my brother Bruce.

One day, Bruce sent me a text that read, "I just heard k.d. lang's version of 'Hallelujah' that she did at the opening for the Olympics. I love how she does that song, but it made me cry because I remembered when you sang it. And I love how you do that song even more than when k.d. lang does it." This caught me off guard. For one, it's rather difficult to think of me singing something that would even come close to touching the incomparable voice of k.d. lang. But more importantly, I knew for a fact that I'd never sung that song before.

Bruce and I went back and forth for a while, me insisting I'd never sung it, him insisting I had. He said he remembered it clearly—that he cried when I sang it, and that he still tears up every time he thinks about it. This continued for months and years, and eventually it just became one of those things. I stopped telling him I hadn't sung it because he was completely convinced otherwise.

One day, some years later, my friend Summer asked me to sing at the funeral of her ex-husband's grandma. She also asked if I would sing "Hallelujah." I said I would, and so I started working on it.

I sent Bruce a text that said, "Hey, I'm finally learning 'Hallelujah'! I'm going to send you a clip of it." I used my phone to make a video of me singing it, but when I tried to send it to him, it wouldn't go through as the file was too big. I tried to send just pieces of the video, but every attempt failed. There was no way I could get the song to him. *Well, that's weird*, I thought. I told him I'd have to come over and sing it for him, and he said it would be nice to hear it again. We went back and forth about that for a while, and then we moved on.

Just before the celebration of life, Summer's family asked to change the song to "Amazing Grace." I was happy to oblige, and I thought to myself how nice it was that I'd finally learned "Hallelujah" regardless. Summer and I sang together—our voices blend beautifully, and it is great to sing with someone you love so much. We then sat to listen to the beautiful eulogy that was given by the grandma's brother. It was beautifully done, full of intimate and joyful memories.

As I was watching him speak, my mind started to wander, as it often does. I thought, *Wow, I wonder what it is like to give a eulogy for a brother or sister. I can't even imagine what it's like to lose one, let alone sit up there and give this eulogy.*

As my mind continued to drift, I thought, Gosh, I wonder which one of us will die first. It was kind of an odd thing to be thinking about. I decided that since Bruce was a non-smoking, non-drinking vegan, he was unlikely to go first. But if he did, I would sing "Hallelujah" for him. I laughed to myself, thinking about how many times we had gone back and forth about that song.

The eulogy ended, and then I waited as my friend visited with relatives. She asked if I needed to leave, but I told her to go ahead and enjoy this time with family. It was a beautiful celebration of life, and I just wanted her to soak in every moment she could.

As I sat there, my mind once again wandered. Mum had passed nine months earlier, and I thought about what it is like to process death and grieve. Once again, I thought about who would do whose eulogy and all of those things. After my friend finished visiting with her relatives, we left and had a beautiful chat on the drive back about love and loss and family.

Later that night, our friend Kate came over for dinner. David, Kate, and I spent some time just chatting about our days and about life in general, and just as we were about to sit down for dinner, the phone rang. I looked at the call display and I saw it was Bruce's number. I thought to myself, *That's weird, he never phones the home number.* Figuring that whatever he wanted to talk about could wait, I didn't pick up and instead sent him a quick text that I had company over and would call him tomorrow, or he could call me later if he needed to talk.

Immediately, the home phone rang again. That was when I knew something was up. I answered the phone right away this time and found myself speaking to my sister-in-law Neva. She was calling to tell me that suddenly, unexpectedly, Bruce had passed away. I later learned he had an abdominal aortic aneurysm. He was gone in an instant.

"No one ever told me that grief felt so like fear."

— C. S. Lewis

It felt like the oxygen was being sucked from my lungs. I couldn't believe what she was saying. It couldn't possibly be true. It was so hard to catch my breath, and the walls began closing in around me. I just wanted to text him and for us to make inappropriate jokes. I wanted to see him. I wanted her to stop saying these things to me. I wanted to hold her and hug her. I asked if she wanted me to come over; she said no, her brother was on his way.

The next morning, I stood looking out across the water, still stunned and finding it hard to catch my breath. I couldn't believe he was gone. In that moment, a calming presence came over me and I somehow felt or heard Bruce's voice in my heart. He said, "Hey Sis, don't worry about me. Please just make sure Neva is okay. Don't forget about her, okay? Stay in touch with her, she is going to need you." And then I was alone again.

I did what my brother asked and spent a lot of time with Neva over the next weeks and months. We grieved together, and it was a very powerful experience for me. Neva was good at grieving—when her dad had passed, she had joined support groups and read a lot about how to grieve properly so that you can actually go on living. Now that she had lost her husband of over thirty-five years, she was making use of this information once more, and I was learning from it. I am so grateful for Neva and how she fully embraced me and her grief. She is a kind, brave, amazing woman, and I know I would not have allowed myself to experience that level of honesty and grief had it not been for her.

Bruce didn't want a funeral, but Neva and I needed to do something for us. So, we decided to hold a small service. Neva asked if I would do the eulogy and sing two songs, one of them being "Oh Danny Boy." That song had been played at a memorial for Bruce's best friend the year before, and Bruce had played that song every day since.

I already knew what the second song needed to be.

The service was held at a beautiful place that my brother Jamie and sister-in-law Lilac were caretakers for. Once everyone had gathered, I got up and spoke for a while, then sang "Oh, Danny Boy." I spoke a little bit more, and then I finally sang "Hallelujah" for my brother, with Jamie playing guitar alongside me.

I have done many funerals and celebrations of life in my life through my work as a minister, and it was always an honour to be invited into such a sacred space. However, it's a very different thing to do a eulogy and sing for someone you know—it's much more difficult to detach a little bit so that you can do the task at hand. In this case, it was especially difficult to sing this song that Bruce and I had so often discussed. I closed my eyes because I was fighting back tears. I didn't want to break down weeping; I wanted to be able to do this thing for my family and for my brother.

Afterwards many, many people came and said, "That was so amazing. What happened when you sang that song?" I wasn't sure what they meant.

Later, I finally was told what people were talking about. Stella, my brother's beautiful Bouvier, had been laying on a big doggy bed throughout the service. She had a brace on her leg to help her recover from a torn ACL, along with several medical conditions that compromised her mobility. While I was singing, she got up even though it was painful for her and she was very unstable on her feet, and she stared at the space just to the right of me. Apparently, she then kept walking around me and sniffing into the air as I sang. Several people told me that Stella must have seen or sensed Bruce, and that it was a powerful experience for them.

Personally, I didn't notice any of that. I was just completely overwhelmed with a sense of the presence of my brother, and I wanted to love on him and gift him, his bride, and our family with this very special song.

Later that night, when I was either sleeping or in a dreamlike state, the truth of what happened came to me. Somehow, my brother was given a glimpse of me singing that song

In the end, all I know is that on that day, the visible spoke of the invisible, the natural spoke of the spiritual, and somehow my brother saw me singing at his memorial years before it happened. That is why he cried every time he heard the song. It was not a feeling of loss that he cried over, but a feeling of deep, deep love between us.

at his celebration of life. Time is linear to us here on earth, but I think that is not really how it works. Science, physics, and many, many spiritual teachings say that time always was and always will be—that it is infinite, and infinity suggests something very different than a straight line. I don't know how it all works, and I have to admit that it messes a bit with my own theology of what I thought I knew. However, everything that I have ever known has always been up for grabs. I used to cling to my beliefs, holding them tightly because I didn't want anyone to try to move, shake, or alter them in any way. Now, I hold my beliefs in a more open-handed fashion, allowing them to shift with my experiences and any new information that comes my way. I want to process the events of my life with critical thinking rather than preconceived notions.

In the end, all I know is that on that day, the visible spoke of the invisible, the natural spoke of the spiritual, and somehow my brother saw me singing at his memorial years before it happened. That is why he cried every time he heard the song. It was not a feeling of loss that he cried over, but a feeling of deep, deep love between us.

This experience gave me so much hope that life and death involve so much more than I could ever imagine. It showed me that death is clearly not the end, and that there are beautiful mysteries that invite us in if we are open to the possibilities. I also found some peace in knowing that however all of this works, it is so much more than I ever dreamed of.

One of my favorite scriptures from the Bible is 1 Corinthians 2:9: "The eye has never seen, the ears never heard and the mind has never even imagined all that God has for those who love him." And I think that this experience was a little taste of that truth. It was a beautiful gift, and I am forever grateful for it.

Part 4

Building Community

19

Liz's Story

"Owning our story and loving ourselves through that process is the bravest thing we'll ever do."

Brené Brown

Throughout this book, I have been sharing lessons I have learned through my own experiences. There are, however, many other people who have shared part of their journeys with me, and their experiences have taught me important lessons as well. I have some amazing friends who have also learned and are learning to live with the impact of trauma in their lives. They have done this with courage and strength and have allowed me to share a little of their experiences, including how enjoying creative pursuits, finding a purpose, and living from a place of gratitude has brought them through some very dark times. I am humbled and grateful that they have trusted me with their stories.

Years ago, an amazing woman I was just getting to know was diagnosed with amyotrophic lateral sclerosis (ALS), also known as Lou Gehrig's disease. This is a horrific disease that attacks the nerves involved in muscle control, resulting in a slow descent toward paralysis and death. Liz was a wonderful person. She was a dog lover; she and her husband

had two big fluffy Newfoundland dogs. She had been a chef, a food critic, a blogger, and an author, and she had lots of plans for her upcoming retirement. Instead, she and her husband were faced with the unthinkable.

There was so much that was hard about her last years and months and weeks, but one of the wonderful things was the meeting of the big dog ladies. I was blessed to be included in this incredible group of women who visited Liz and loved on her. We dressed up for Halloween, we went on walks to raise money for ALS awareness and research, and we had luncheons and Christmas parties. Through it all, Liz showed incredible courage and humour among the raw, vulnerable truth of her experience.

Liz loved to write, and she was amazing at it, filling pages with humour and honesty. As someone who was still struggling to write my first book at the time, she was an inspiration to me. We would talk about her cookbooks and about her first novel, a mystery, which she was working on when she became ill. Liz told me, "Write the books! Everyone should write at least one book." I like to think that Liz is smiling now, cheering me on.

In addition to her writing, Liz used her creativity to build a little miniature house that she filled with beautiful furnishings, enjoying crafting while she still had use of her hands. In the times when our thoughts are filled with fear and confusion, creativity can be a welcome distraction.

I wrote a poem about all of these amazing women and what I saw as I looked at them—looked at us. "When I look at you I see" was a term I learned when I was studying with Streams ministry, and it reminded us to look at a person and see all that they were and all that they are capable of being. One of the women and her husband made beautiful driftwood sailboats for each of us so that we could attach a message for Liz, and I attached this poem to mine. Liz lined the boats up along her mantel, and they brought her so much joy.

We were each given our boat back after Liz passed away, and I treasure mine. It reminds me of those days—some dark, all filled with *love*.

Driftwood Boat by Alison Perry-Davies

When I look at You I see...

BY ALISON PERRY-DAVIES

When I look at you I see
Beauty
strength
Wondrous
Warrior women
Generations
Deep

Voices loud
Shattering barriers
Carrying hope
Awakening dreams
Breathing passions
Consciously exploring
All we are designed for

Gentle
Powerful
Nurturing
Exploring
Conquering
Loving
Courageous, All

When I look at you I see
Dreams realized
Lives thriving
Creation exploding
Personal mythology challenged
Limitless potential

A reason to believe

Inspiration
Compassion
Community
Weeping
Laughing
Accepting
Divine, All

When I look at you I see
All that is possible
Inside you
Inside me

20

The Frantastic Four

"Some people are worth melting for."
Olaf, *Frozen*

For me and Dave, building community has always been a big part of our lives. In the spirit of community, we value close friendships and have a close group of friends we call the "Frantastic Four," a small group of people—all artists who have learned to heal through creativity—who have become family. There is my dear husband Dave and his three "wives": myself, Francis, and Kate. Three of the four of us have been diagnosed with PTSD and have learned to find ways to exist and thrive. We are kind and gentle with each other, and also honest. Honesty spoken in love is a wonderful thing, and we have earned the right to be that way with each other. What we share within this "sacred bubble" is always safe from judgements or unkindness. It is a space where we can share our deepest thoughts, our silliness, our seriousness. We will brainstorm about our ideas, hopes, and dreams until they are ready to become a reality. Our sacred bubble is a place where we are all completely free to be fully who we are without feeling a need to hold in our stomachs, watch our words, guard our hearts, or

The Portal by Francis Dick

sit up straight. In this group, we know we are loved.

Francis is one of the most brilliant artists I know; her creativity and talents seem limitless She does everything from paintings to carving wood, creating jewelry out of gold and silver, writing plays, singing traditional songs as a Hamatsa, and on and on. Francis is a contemporary Native artist and a member of the Kwakwaka'wakw Nation, born into the Musqamakw Dzawadaenutw Band (the four tribes of Kingcome Inlet). She is a descendant of the supernatural Wolf, Kawadelekala, who was the first of the Kingcome people.

Like many stories, though, we are coming into it in the last third of the book. The darkness in which this incredible life was developed began very early, and the courageous being of light that emerged from such awfulness would seem to me an urban legend if I did not know her so well.

At the age of five, Francis was ripped from her family and put into a residential school where she suffered unthinkable abuse and trauma. Then, while living in a community with widespread generational trauma, she was also abused by people she should have been able to trust. As if that wasn't enough, she also lost her mom at a very young age.

Francis learned early on that there were no safe places and no safe people. She kept most people at a distance, with a few notable exceptions—she was especially close to her youngest brother, Jesse. She began her career as a social worker after graduating from the University of Victoria, but she quickly realized that her true calling was to honour her natural artistic talents. Her first Northwest Coast painting, Kawadelekala, was created and then published as a way to honour her grandmother's life and spirit after her death in December of 1985. Jesse took his own life four months later, so she created her second Northwest Coast painting as a way to honour him.

The pain of losing Jesse was the catalyst for Francis to begin her journey of self-discovery through her art. I have watched over the years as the darkness has come and tried to claim her; it haunts and taunts her, looking for ways to come in and take over. Consistently, I have witnessed our dear friend push back with love, kindness, and creativity. Over and over again, she chooses light over darkness, love over hate, kindness over cruelty, and mercy over judgement.

Francis and I have had many long talks, and on days we are both struggling we will share the rawness of it all. Francis' answer is always to create. When she is overwhelmed by yet another death, she paints. When she is plagued by memories and nightmares that refuse to

Handmade Smudge Fans by "Auntie Kate" Roland

leave her alone, she will "trek" and carve, always finding someone to build up and honour. Having been treated so unkindly, Francis finds ways to act in the opposite spirit: with grace, generosity, and kindness.

It may seem I am exaggerating, but I can assure you I am not. I have so often found that those who have known such cruelty find ways to show grace as they heal; it becomes who they are rather than how they are.

Francis' story is one I want to read over and over again. Each page is filled with pain and tragedy, and yet there is also triumph. I love and adore her and am constantly blown away that she is one of my dearest friends. I am grateful to the loving creator for placing us together. You can find her art in places like Oscardo Canada. Her Facebook artist page is The Art of Francis Dick, and her website is francisdick.com.

Another member of our "sacred bubble" is our dear Kate. Kate is an amazing singer, songwriter, storyteller, historian and passionate speaker and teacher of her Hawaiian heritage. When Kate is not on stage singing or teaching, she is creating incredible smudge fans and other artwork.

Kate grew up on Salt Spring Island with her beautiful family, whose heritage is Hawaiian, Coast Salish, and a wee bit of Scottish just for fun. She is the youngest out of eight kids—five girls and three boys—and she grew up surrounded by loud laughter, fishing trips, hard work, songs and stories with her brothers and sisters, and lessons from her Uncle Paul, who taught her so much about their rich history.

Kate has wonderful stories about life on Salt Spring as a child, about working up north in pubs when she was young, and then about the thirty-plus years she spent touring as Auntie Kate and the Uncles of Funk and all the wild and wonderful adventures she had along the way.

Within our group, Kate is our rock. It isn't so much that she had things easy, though she came from a very solid family who all seemed to know their place of importance, both in the family and in the world. Kate is one of those people who seems to be able to stay the course no matter what storms come her way. She always tells me that I "need to be Switzerland," which is a reminder that I don't need to have an opinion on absolutely everything. Neutrality is just fine at times, and often it is preferred.

Kate keeps her hands busy creating, and she says that is how she remains steady. Kate has certainly experienced pain in her life, and she has always gotten through it by pouring herself into creating songs, art, smudge fans, button blankets, decorations, and lovely handmade gifts.

As for Dave, he was raised around strong immigrant families. His mom's parents were from Slovakia, his dad and grandfather were born in Wales, and his grandmother was born in Italy. He was very close to his grandparents and learned an amazing work ethic from them.

Dave comes from his own understanding of trauma and pain through his experiences growing up as well as the more than thirty years he spent serving in the military. He tends to be someone who stays mostly to himself, except for at certain times and with certain people. This safe little group of four is just perfect for him.

Dave is one of the most disciplined people any of us know. He is a musician and a model builder and finds ways to make life work for him through quiet reflection. He had an amazing relationship with Gilly, our beautiful blue heeler rescue, who became his PTSD support dog. Losing her to cancer was very hard on him. It is my great honour to be sharing life with him, and we have come a very long way together.

The Frantastic Four have been, and continue to be, an enormous source of support in my life. I hope that everyone has a group of people like this in their life—people who are safe and encouraging and who they can grow with. I know that not everyone has support like this, and if you are reading this and you do not have friendships or a community where you feel safe from the cares of this world, I suggest finding ways to meet and build your own team. I strongly believe that building relationships are an important part of our mental, physical, emotional, and spiritual health. I also know that this seems like it's easier said than done. However, once we start to believe something and visualize it, we attract whatever that may be into our lives—even people. So, take some time to visualize the type of people you want to meet, and then put yourself in situations where you can meet them. Community groups, non-profit organizations, sports teams, or any type of place where people gather can all be great resources for meeting others in a safe environment.

Once you find a few new friends you think can become a support system for you, take the time to build trust with them. The Frantastic Four did not start out as the close-knit group it is today; we learned to trust each other one dinner at a time. It takes time and effort to build a community, but once you do, your life changes in the best kind of way.

21

Frankie's Story

"It's the friends you can call at 4 a.m. that matter."
Marlene Dietrich

In 1995, I met Beth at a board of directors meeting for the Military Family Resource Centre at the Canadian Forces Base in Esquimalt. Beth and I had several things in common, including being married to military members and raising children who were living with some cognitive challenges. We hit it off right away. Eventually, we realized that our husbands were deployed on different ships but at the same time, and that there was going to be a naval exercise with some leave happening in Hawaii. We all met up there together, and the four of us soon became great friends.

When I met Beth's husband Frankie, I could not help but love him. He has a boisterous laugh, a larger-than-life attitude, and a heart so big I can barely fit the description of it within these pages. He can be crude and rude and completely inappropriate—he has no time for filters. He has seen things that no one should see, done things he doesn't want to remember, and is trapped in a mind that refuses to forget.

Fireworks by Alison Perry-Davies

Inspired by friends coming home from deployment with PTSD who can no longer be around fireworks. The paintings are a series of fireworks with poppies. I wanted to give them a safe way to see fireworks again and to honour them for their service.

Frankie was a proud serving member of the Canadian Armed Forces, as was his brother and their father before them. Doing this mattered to him greatly. He, like so many others, believed so strongly in defending his country and standing for others who were unable to do so. He followed that vision, and it took him to war-torn places where he lost friends, lost time, and lost hope. If you talk to Frankie about his deployments though, he talks about the perfumes he bought, the food he tried, the beers he tasted, and the time he got chased down the beach and into the water by some adorable monkeys. He talks about the women he saw and jokes about what could have been with little miss "me love you long time" if he wasn't married, all through his thunderous laughter.

Percolating beneath the surface, though—beneath the laughter and the stories and the beer—was a place so dark that even this larger-than-life man could not find the will or the courage to enter.

After a few deployments, Frankie came home with parts of who he had once been scattered around the globe. With a confirmed case of PTSD and a decreasing ability to cope, he was medically released from the Canadian Forces and his world crashed down around him—a medical release for PTSD can be a very difficult experience for a member who does not want to stop serving. He drank hard. He curled in a ball at the sound of fireworks. He tried laughing louder than the voices in his head that haunted him day in and day out. He attempted to take his life. I would say our dear friend was lost for a long time.

Percolating beneath the surface, though beneath the laughter and the stories and the beer—was a place so dark that even this larger-than-life man could not find the will or the courage to enter.

Over time, Frankie found ways to feel alive again. He went through counselling, group programs, and treatment centres to find healing, but one of the ways he found hope was building models of military equipment—through them, he seemed to find a connection to his service and military life. The models were meticulously detailed, and Frankie would spend hours and hours painting and assembling them. It seemed that putting the models together helped him to put himself back together; the time spent building and creating brought a welcome relief from the chatter in his head.

Other ways that Frankie seemed to find joy and meaning was taking walks in the bush with his Rottweiler Buddy at his side or playing his drum kit, which was set up right in the middle of all his models.

Frankie is both kind and kind of crazy, and I love that about him. I have seen him fight to find himself and his place in this world, and I have seen the role that creativity—whether that be building models, playing his drums, or enjoying creation while out fishing—has played in this process.

Thank you for your service, Frankie, and welcome home.

22

Ron's Story

"I've learned that people will forget what you said, people will forget what you did, but people will never forget how you made them feel."

Maya Angelou

I met Ron over twenty years ago when I started working at a group home for adults living with autism and other cognitive challenges. He is a black man who was born in Louisiana in 1944, where he was raised mostly by his mama (grandmother) and his mom. We worked together for over four years, often on double shifts. At night, when our clients were asleep, Ron would tell me (at my request) about his experiences growing up black and poor in the South. I learned so much from Ron, and he is a dear friend to this day.

Ron told me about the "black churches" and how he and his friends would get into all kinds of shenanigans when they were kids, like trying to drop things into ladies' purses from the church balcony. He talked about the music and the joy and the adventures they would have in church. He told me about the bread his mama baked—how that smell filled the air and how he would be so excited for it. He told me about the joyful, happy times, and how grateful he was to make it out as so many did not. He told me that when we go visit someday, I should not

say anything about the iced tea not being very iced because people might not have fridges.

He told me about attending the first integrated schools and how people spit and screamed at them for being black. When I asked him if he was scared, he told me, "Well, mostly I was so excited I was going to be able to learn." This was Ron's way; he was always so grateful and kind. I told him I wasn't sure I could be so grateful after such unkindness had been done to me, but Ron was clear that you have to be grateful and move on or it would eat you alive—"it" being the pain, hatred, and bitterness that racism spews and spreads.

One time, in 2008, I went to a conference in Texas and met a black man while I was there. His name escapes me now, but he was a lovely person, and we chatted a few times. One day, I was driving from my hotel to the church where the conference was being held and saw this man walking down the road, still a few miles from the church. Now, I am from Canada so perhaps it seemed hotter to me than it did to him, but it was over eighty degrees Fahrenheit and he had to have already walked a few miles. I didn't want to leave him to walk the rest of the way, so I pulled over and offered him a ride to the church. He really did not want to accept the offer, but I wouldn't take no for an answer. After quite some time, he finally relented. He didn't talk much on the drive, other than to thank me before he got out.

When I got home to Canada, Ron and I talked about the conference and all that had happened. I mentioned my experience with this gentleman to him, and Ron's response shocked me. He said, "Ali, what were you thinking? This may be 2008, but he is still black, and Texas is still in the South! You were a white woman with a black man, and he knew that if you took anything he did or said wrong and reported it, or if someone saw you both and didn't like that... you just don't understand what that could mean for him!" And he was right, I didn't understand. It had never occurred to me that there would be a problem for him or me; I just

All Things New by Alison Perry-Davies

Inspired by friends coming home from deployment with PTSD who can no longer be around fireworks. The paintings are a series of fireworks with poppies. I wanted to give them a safe way to see fireworks again and to honour them for their service.

wanted to offer him a ride because it was a long walk in the heat. But for Ron, his experiences of racism and the reality of what could have happened were still so clear. Being saturated in the generational trauma from centuries of abuse, slavery, and racism had left him with a deep knowing of the things people are capable of, which I can never fully comprehend.

Ron completed two tours in Vietnam from 1967-1969, and they left a significant mark on him. One day, Ron and I were standing outside at work and a car backfired as it was driving down the street. Before I could even register what had happened, Ron had dropped to the ground. Once he realized the source of the noise, he simply got up, brushed himself off, and said, "Just some stuff from over there." Ron never called it Vietnam or 'Nam or anything I have ever heard in movies or TV shows. He just called it "over there."

Ron invited Dave and I over to his place one night and brought out a photo album from that time. He told us he could still smell "over there" when he looked at the pages. This is a testament to the power of triggers and trauma. Many decades after his time in Vietnam, that place still held such power over him that he was filled with the smells of it when he looked at the pictures.

Like many people living with PTSD, Ron self-medicated with alcohol to cope with life. He always made it to work on time and never complained about hangovers, but it was clear he wasn't doing well. One day, I finally said to him "You look like crap, and you smell like yesterday's booze. Get it together, friend!"

The next day, Ron came into work and informed me he had quit smoking and drinking, just like that. He said that no one else had ever cared enough to speak to him that way, and he trusted me and believed me when I said he wasn't doing well. I expressed my surprise that he was quitting both at once, and his response impacted me greatly. "Yep. I can do this. I'm doing it just like I did when I was over there. I know I can do a day at a time, and if I can't do a day, I can do an hour or a minute. Some days, when I was over there, I was so scared that I had to do just one second at a time. When I got through that one second, I would tell myself, 'See, you made it through that second, now you can do the next one.' I did that for over two years, and it worked. I made it." Today, thirteen years later, Ron has never smoked or drank again.

I have remembered those words and have relied on them myself when I am going through very challenging times. I remind myself that I have known anxiety and depression and the terror waves of trauma in my life—that I made it through then, and I will again. This is a wonderful thing to remind ourselves of when facing challenges.

One day I will never forget is the day Barack Obama was first elected president of the United States. Ron had come over to our house to watch the results, and he was telling me about the people who showed up to vote and what a historical moment this was. Now, I'm going be honest with you that there are times when I learn something that deeply resonates with me, and that those lessons are usually around thoughts that I am somewhat ashamed to admit I once had. In this case, I am white enough and privileged enough that there were still places in me that thought, *Why do they need to keep saying that he is black? Why can't they just talk about his merits as a man? As a politician? Why can't they focus on what he will bring to their country?*

That day, my dear friend Ron sat on our couch and said to me through tears, "I would never have imagined that my mama's son, who was a slave—a slave! Do you understand me? My great grandmother was a slave! And she and my mama raised me! And I was alive to see a black man elected as the president of the United States of America, and HE, that black man, was elected while my mama's son is still alive!" He wept and wept, and I wept with him, shedding tears that I could not have understood lived within me. How blessed am I that someone so exquisite and so kind considers me a friend, and that he shared that beautiful truth with me in a way that I could finally see and understand even a taste of something so sacred. It was not mine, and still it was shared with me.

The most important lesson I learned from Ron is to be grateful for what I have. Gratitude is one of the powerful tools that I now use to keep myself on track and healthy in my mind, body, spirit, and emotions. A gratitude journal is a wonderful way to keep my mind centred and aware of all that is beautiful in my life. Gently recalling all that I am grateful for upon waking in the morning and before going to bed at night is one of the ways that I stay balanced. It reminds me of the scripture, "Whatever is good and pure and lovely, think on these things." And I can truly say that I am grateful for Ron.

23

Auntie Arlene's Story

"You're braver than you believe,
stronger than you seem, and smarter than you think."
A.A. Milne, *Winnie the Pooh*

Births, deaths, and illnesses of all sorts can be stressful or even traumatic, depending on how things happen and how we are able to process them. Any time spent in a hospital can feel rather scary for many people, as was the case for my sweet auntie.

Auntie Arlene—who was not an auntie by blood, but rather Mum's dear friend—was a real character. She was also a nurse, and if you have any of those types in your life, you'll know they are a wonderfully wild bunch with big hearts and crazy ways. Or at least, the ones who hung out at our place were. Mum and Auntie Arlene shared a love for bingo, garage sales, canning pickles, playing cards, and drinking wine. *Especially* drinking wine

Sadly, Auntie Arlene eventually developed cancer on her tongue, and while she was a strong woman with attitude for days, this took her to her knees. She was terrified. They were going to have to surgically remove a portion of her tongue, and they weren't sure how long it would take her to be able to speak afterward, if she was able to speak at all. We went to the hospital together, and I stayed with her until she was taken in. As you can imagine, it was a really hard morning for her as she didn't know what she would wake up to.

As soon as she went in, I went to her room and took a look around. I knew she needed to be in a place that looked inviting, and hospital rooms don't tend to be that way. I went out and bought the brightest yellow things that I could find—yellow balloons, yellow flowers, and a little teddy bear with a bright yellow raincoat and yellow boots. I filled her room with as much yellow and love as I could fit into it. Bringing colour, love, and humour to a space is another form of creativity, and it has carried me through many difficult times.

Hours later, when they brought Arlene back to her bright yellow room, I sat beside her and just sang "Amazing Grace" over her. She didn't have much of a relationship with God or any sort of religious background, but oh, did she love that song. I stopped after a while, and she opened her eyes, looked up at me, and said with her stubby new tongue, "Thing it a den."

She could talk! Sure, it was lispy, and it sounded a bit like her mouth was full of cotton candy, but she could talk, and I could understand her. She was saying, "Sing it again," and so I did. I sang it again and again and again.

I slept on the chair beside her bed that night, and every other night throughout her hospital stay. She had been so happy to see the yellow room, so I wanted to do even more to help lift her spirits. There was a big white board on the wall at the end of her bed, and once the staff didn't need all of it for her care, well, I took it over. I drew the motor home she and Uncle Jim owned, and drew the two of them, me, and Mum all going for adventures in it. And of course, I drew her with a stubby little tongue and did all her words in a way that reflected her newfound speech differences. She was howling in laughter, we both were, tears pouring down our cheeks as she told me how mean I was. I called her stubby and we laughed harder still.

Soon she was able to go home, but she was still on chemo. I came over to visit as often as I could, and we would play cards. She once said to me, "You wouldn't be winning all the time if I wasn't so sick," to which I replied, "Oh, poor me, I have cancer and a stubby tongue, playing cards is too hard for me." She had a quick wit and could give them as well as she could take them; I suppose that is how we made it through some pretty rough days.

She told me it scared her when her hair fell out, so I suggested she might take control over when it came off and just shave it. We laughed while I did a really bad job of shaving her head and then laughed even more while we went wig shopping. We laughed and we laughed, and sometimes we cried. The two of us had always been close, and in these last few years we became even closer.

162

I was going to Bible college at the time, and Auntie Arlene decided she wanted to know more about God. She informed me that she didn't want anything fancy, so I bought a children's Bible story book and read it to her. We talked about love and heaven and what might come next. I find that no matter what or who people may have thought they were angry about or at, when they were getting ready to cross to the other side, often the only person they were trying to forgive was themselves. So, we talked about forgiveness and hope and how it was all a really good deal. We shared many stories and songs and tears of sadness and joy.

Some of my greatest lessons in life have been at the bedside of people who are dying; forgiveness, love, humour, and some form of creativity always seem to be present there.

The last time I saw Auntie Arlene alive, I laid on the bed beside her and sang "Amazing Grace." Then she said to me, "Can you hear that?"

"Hear what?" I asked.

"The train," she said. "There is a train coming to pick me up. Do I need a ticket?"

"No Auntie," I told her, "you have everything you need." I smiled as I thought of the old Curtis Mayfield song "People Get Ready." I felt at peace knowing she was ready. She passed away a few days later.

Some of my greatest lessons in life have been at the bedside of people who are dying; forgiveness, love, humour, and some form of creativity always seem to be present there. I spent so much of my life afraid of death and dying, afraid to really look closely at the process. But over time, I discovered that when I was sharing with a person who was facing their own mortality in a very real way, I was able to experience such an incredible peace-filled honesty.

I think it important to realize that when we are supporting someone who is dying, we may go through a wide range of emotions that goes beyond anything we might have imagined.

For example, I wasn't prepared to feel frightened about what Auntie Arlene was experiencing physically, emotionally, or spiritually. I was also surprised by the shame I felt for spending so much time thinking *oh my gosh, I don't want this to happen to me.* I now have come to understand that this is a natural part of the process. Once we have walked closely alongside a person in the final steps of their life on this side of that mystical veil, it becomes impossible to go back to the way things were. Our thoughts, our vision, and our views are all forever changed.

From these experiences, I have learned that people can go through things that terrify them and still find ways to love and laugh and learn and grow. I have learned that once death becomes inevitable, some people are able to somehow submit to that and find peace while others seem to struggle—regret or worry about what will happen to those left behind appears to have a lot to do with that. This was another lesson that reminded me to find ways to heal all that I can heal right here, right now—my relationships, my body, my physical health, my mental health, my spiritual health, my emotional health, every aspect of my being.

See you on the other side, Auntie.

24

Memories of Mum

"Youth fades; love droops; the leaves of friendship fall;
A mother's secret hope outlives them all."
Oliver Wendell Holmes

One of the effects of the trauma I experienced is that I struggled with relationships for most of my life. I felt afraid, alone, attacked, judged, and misunderstood, and that makes for a very unstable base to build anything healthy, safe, and meaningful from. One relationship I struggled with for years was my relationship with my mum. I know, I know, mothers and daughters, right? But we really struggled, and it took me so many years and modalities of healing to understand how we are often too afraid of being hurt to trust others while also being completely unaware of this fact. We judge ourselves so harshly, and anyone who might remind us of that can trigger all our self-hate and self-rejection.

Don't get me wrong, Mum and I had many wonderful times together. I adored her and she adored me, but we also had conflicts and arguments. There was a bit of a storm swirling around in the shadows, never really spoken of. Today, I can see how much she worried about me, and how she didn't want to see me make mistakes she had made. I see how much she wanted to spare me from taking a more difficult path than I needed to.

Mum had experienced significant trauma and abandonment in her own life, and that of course coloured and shaped the way she saw the world. But there was so much more to her than that—so much I want you to know about her. I want you to know how strong she was, and how kind. How she was intelligent and witty and fun to be with. How she loved me fiercely and did so much to make my life great. How she loved to learn and loved being a registered nurse. How much she wanted me to become a nurse—oh, how I wish I had listened to her.

Mum had a way of making everyone feel like they were her favourite—her kids, her friends, her patients, and the people who cared for her in the end. Everyone felt like her favourite, and somehow, we all were. She also had a way of making everything an adventure. She taught us about dreaming and having hope, about respect and strength, and about the importance of family.

Mum not only loved being a nurse, but she was also excellent at it. She loved the people she cared for, and that shone through in everything she did. Mum occasionally told the story of a man who needed to be sedated, and how several of the staff were trying and failing to calm him down enough for him to allow them to give him the injection he required. Things had gotten a bit out of control. She asked the rest of the staff to leave, and then she calmly sat down beside the man and said, "You know, they are going to give you this shot. If you will let me, I will give it to you so you don't have to deal with them being all over you. Would that be okay?" And of course, he let her.

Mum had a rule about dinners where guests would be coming: she always said that we should always put out an extra place setting. She said that if we didn't need it we could put it away, but if someone showed up, she wanted them to know we had a place for them—she didn't want them to feel like an afterthought. She always gave a voice to the voiceless.

After Mum was diagnosed with Parkinson's and vascular dementia, she lived with Dave and I for many years as her ability to care for herself declined. Before she had to go into complex care, she ended up in the hospital for a while. Every day I would go in, put her into her wheelchair, and take her outside to walk and talk. On bad days she wasn't very aware of what was happening, but on good days it was like she was back to her old self.

One such day, we sat down during our walk to enjoy a coffee and muffin. Mum was looking so cute, all bundled up in her cozy blanket, a gentle breeze blowing her now wispy hair. She looked up at me and said, "I just want you to know you took amazing care of me. I wanted to tell you that now in case I get worse and forget and can't tell you. I don't know how you knew how to do all of this. I am an RN, for goodness sakes, and I didn't take as good care of my mum as you did me. How did you know to do all of that?"

We chatted a bit about what my career had been for the last few decades and the things I learned along the way. Then, as if this day was not wonderful enough already, something amazing happened. Mum leaned over, held my face in her hands, and just stared at me all teary-eyed. "My gosh," she said, "you are so beautiful. Why did I never know that before?"

I smiled and gently said, "Oh Mum, it's okay. How could you have seen that? I reminded you of you, and you hated yourself so much that you couldn't see beauty in me. You would have had to see it in yourself, and you weren't ready yet."

Mum thought for a moment, then kissed my forehead and said, "I guess you're right. When did you get so smart?"

I responded, "If you think I'm smart, you should meet my mum."

"Give the children love, more love and still more love –

and the common sense will come by itself."

— **Astrid Lindgren,** *Pippi Longstocking*

Somehow, it had happened. Without fanfare or celebration, with no fuss or no muss, I was healing. *We* were healing! All the pain, all the rejection, and everything else that had tormented us was gone. As we had matured and healed, all the things we struggled with fell away. We learned to love ourselves, which then allowed us to fully love each other. Self-love was always the key, and that took healing. All we had to do now was bask in the love.

As has so often come up in this book, creativity also seemed to play a role in the way Mum moved through the word. Throughout her life, Mum loved to play the piano—I can remember times during my childhood when she would suddenly go and start playing a song. Looking back as an adult, I imagine that on very difficult days, of which there were many for her, the piano would offer her some solace. In the last several years of her life, Mum began exploring creativity in many ways. She wrote children's stories. She created beautiful abstract pieces using felt pens and pencil crayons. She loved to come up with new recipes and would give these yummy creations as gifts in little containers with fancy bows. Her life had been full of so many struggles, and it was so wonderful to see her find creative outlets for all that was inside her.

The recreation director at the facility Mum was in had a wonderful way of opening up opportunities for the residents to be creative. One of the things she did was attaining a grant for a project called "Life is Art." This project included the creation of a DVD, a book, and a CD, and it was a beautiful way for everyone to create together. The CD portion was created by a wonderful singer-songwriter named Paul O'Brien, who came in a few times a week for a full year to collect the stories of the wonderful residents which he then turned into songs. It was amazing. I was deeply honoured to sing one of those songs on the recording produced by the incomparable Joby Baker, which was an incredible experience. Mum loved the song so much, she always asked for me to put it on. I am so grateful that I was able to share that with her.

In her last few days, Mum was in a deep sleep. I sat with her and told her over and over how much I loved her, and that we were all going to be okay. I sang "You Are My Sunshine" over her so many times, each time remembering how she would sing it to my brothers and I when we were little. I was with her when she took her last breath, singing over her with my hand on her chest. I kissed her and told her thanks. Then, as if from a movie, I sang the line "In the arms of the angels, fly away," and that was it. She was gone.

We held a small celebration of life for her, at which I gave a eulogy. My friend Beth, who is Metis, read a Native prayer while my friend Kate gave a Hawaiian blessing. I laughed, remembering another night when Kate had given my mom a blessing. She and I had been out for a walk and a few glasses of wine, and we decided to walk all the way to visit Mum and have a wee bit of Kahlua with her. Oh, how she loved Kahlua! Anyways, Kate spoke a Hawaiian blessing over Mum that night, and Mum gushed about how beautiful it was before turning to me and saying, "What is that?" Revisiting that memory made it feel like Mum was right there, and it felt wonderful. We had appies and prosecco as we laughed and talked about so many memories. Francis was there too—she had gifted Mum a beautiful print of one of her original artworks for Mum's ninetieth birthday, and Mum had been so happy.

I am so teary as I type this; I miss her so much. I just want one more card game, one more chance to make pickles together, one more road trip, one more bingo game, one more night where we laugh until our sides ache. Just one more. I am so very grateful for healing and hope and forgiveness and all that brought us to the place we were before she passed over to the other side.

I had been victim-shaming my body, and now I was determined to rid myself of this toxic load.
I am so grateful for my body, which has been through so much and carried me through so much, and I asked my body's forgiveness.

Even to this day, I still learn lessons that originate from my mum or connect me to her in some way. Recently, I took an online course on photography—well, mostly on body image and selfies and self-love. Part of my journey around learning to be at peace with who I am has involved working on my issues around body image. My sweet mum had often said some rather unkind words to herself around her face and body and aging, and I knew that I could so easily find myself taking part in that same critical self-talk. While anyone can struggle with this, it seems to mostly be experienced by women, especially women who have experienced sexual trauma. This was something that my mum faced, as did I, though I expressed different criticisms around my own body. In some ways, I rejected my body. I shamed it for not being enough or for being too much, for having stretch marks and scars and any imperfection. I ridiculed and judged my body as if it was somehow not even attached to me, spewing toxic words and thoughts and dismissing all we had been through together. My body had protected me, loved me, nurtured me, cared for me, and yet somehow I had been blaming it, thinking that if I'd been stronger, if I'd been faster, if I'd been prettier, if I'd been uglier… I had been victim-shaming my body, and now I was determined to rid myself of this toxic load. I am so grateful for my body, which has been through so much and carried me through so much, and I asked my body's forgiveness.

As part of this online course, I took a picture of my hands that showed my wrinkles and age spots, and I was inspired to write a poem that celebrated everything my hands had experienced. And as I think of my own hands, I remember the wonderful feeling of my mum's hands resting against my cheeks.

169

These hands...

BY ALISON PERRY-DAVIES

These hands grasped my mum's finger to take my first step…

These hands trembled as they held the wobbling handlebars on the maiden voyage
of my bike without its training wheels…

These hands wiped my little girl tears and clung to my dog when my dad left…

These hands wrote my first song just after my nana passed…

These hands begged my mind to not be afraid to protect my body from unwanted touches…

These hands held pens and pencils and books while I studied…

These hands picked up my first attempt to self-medicate …

These hands have expressed anger and kindness and learned the latter is where they
choose to live…

These hands put the key in the ignition of my new-to-me 1959 Ford Zephyr and took it for a spin…

These hands held the most beautiful girl and boy I had ever seen…

These hands worked hard to provide for the three of us…

These hands held tight when they found a heart they could trust…

These hands have created a home, a safe space, for many….

These hands love to play instruments and paint and write poetry and stories and …

These hands have sat at a desk that helped bring hope to some people that desperately
needed it…

These hands have believed in healing for others…

These hands have scratched bellies of some of the most amazing dogs ever…

These hands have planted gardens and cared for them…

These hands have held their grandbabies and been in awe of creation…

These hands have nourished and cherished too many to count…

These hands have travelled and experienced sacred rituals…

These hands were on my mum's chest as she took her last breath…

These hands have earned every wrinkle and spot; with love…

Photo credit: Dave Davies

Photo credit: Alison Perry-Davies

25

Dad and I Finding Our Way Back

"Fathering is not something perfect men do,
but something that perfects the man."
Frank Pittman

Around the time that Dad told me his cancer had come back, Dave and I had been taking our German shepherd Sammie to a veterinarian on the mainland. She had been diagnosed with stage four lymphoma and was given two weeks to live unless we started aggressive chemotherapy. As a result, I was preoccupied and didn't understand the full extent of what was happening, of what Dad was telling me. I didn't know that my dad was dying—at least not right away.

So, when Dad told me his cancer was back, I said that we didn't really know each other the way I would hope we would—no blaming, just stating the facts—and that I would like to change that. I asked if he would be open to me visiting once a week to just hang out. Dave and I lived on Vancouver Island while my dad lived in the greater Vancouver area, which made regular visits challenging at times. However, we were going to have to bring Sammie to the area for her chemotherapy treatments, so I could easily come see him at those times. He thought this was a great idea. All he had ever wanted was to be closer to his kids; family meant everything to him.

Let me back things up a bit. After our parents' divorced, there were many years where there was a disconnection between Dad and me. He was absent, and that left my brothers and I feeling abandoned. While there were attempts to connect over the years and the two of us still saw each other, it often felt uncomfortable, as these situations can when two people don't know each other very well—it was lacking the ease that comes with a relationship built over time and shared experiences. We were healing still and not really talking openly about things, as many families do, and that needs to happen in order to communicate in a healthy way.

Our visits were sometimes awkward at first; we would sit there in silence at times, trying

---

There is a beautiful thing that can happen when someone is approaching the end of their time on Earth. There is no room for trying to find just the right way to say something—the days of gently sampling ways to hint at your true meaning are gone. This moment, this day, could be the last time we talked, and we have run out of pleasantries and meanderings. Shit just got real.

---

to come up with something to talk about. Most of our early conversations were about Sammie and how worried I was about her—she had cancer, after all!

One day, as Dave and I were heading back to the ferry, my brother John called me and asked me if I knew how sick Dad was. I told him that I had just left, and that Dad was doing great. John said, "No, Alison, he isn't. He's dying. He has been given three to six months to live, and the doctor thinks he will be lucky to get three."

Those words came crashing in, and all I could think was, *What are you saying? Why are you saying this? I just saw him! He didn't say anything about that! I have been visiting him every week; I think I would know if he was dying.*

But he was, in fact, dying, and I didn't know. Now, I did.

The next time I saw my dad, I looked him in the eye and said, "I didn't know, Dad. I didn't know you are dying. I didn't know that the cancer had come back like that. I am so sorry I keep talking about my dog and you are dying." We both sat quietly and exchanged a knowing look.

There is a beautiful thing that can happen when someone is approaching the end of their time on Earth. There is no room for trying to find just the right way to say something—the days of gently sampling ways to hint at your true meaning are gone. This moment, this day, could be the last time we talked, and we have run out of pleasantries and meanderings. Shit just got real.

Our visits began in late 2018, and the news—the actual, factual news—became real to me late January 2019. After that time, I made sure I came over at least once a week, and our conversations became open and awkward and honest and happy and heart-wrenching and scary and confusing and beautiful. We just did what we needed to do to get where we needed to get.

For the first six months of our real visits—the honest ones, as I would say—Dad apologized every time I saw him, sometimes several times, for leaving us when we were kids and for not staying in contact with us much after he left. There were lots of apologies, and lots of me saying, "It's okay, Dad, I've made so many mistakes too." One of the things I have learned in my life is that we all hurt people, and we all make choices that we would give almost anything to take back or do differently. Finding a way to move beyond that is the only way we can find freedom from it.

There is a wonderful, freeing place that comes with the realization that our parents are simply fellow humans trying to find their way through life. They are people who had their own hopes and fears, dreams and pains, tragedies and triumphs. Once this truth becomes clear, everything else kind of falls in place. No matter what they might have done or not done, no matter how personal their actions or words may have felt or how much they hurt, no matter how deep and endless the wound may be or feel, their part in it was as another person on the planet just trying to figure it out. Bit by bit, Dad and I learned to be less uncomfortable with each other, and with ourselves.

When a death is expected and we have time to think and plan and make our way back to each other, there are beautiful opportunities for hope, healing, and love. I watched Dad and

Photo credit: Alison Perry-Davies

Sandy (my stepmom of over fifty years) trying to work out the things that people do in the last stages of their life together. I also observed how amazing my brother Jamie was, bringing Dad to his appointments and making him homemade soup on top of just hanging out with him most days.

During this time, I had been planning a few trips that were now fast approaching. I was turning sixty that September, and I was going to visit Montreal and Old Quebec City with my friend Kate—neither of us had ever been. Dave and I were also planning on going to Hawaii in November, spending one week on Kauai and one week on Maui to celebrate our twenty-fifth wedding anniversary. Dad loved to travel, so every week we would chat about my plans.

One day, Dad said to me, "Look, I don't get a vote in all of this (pointing in a circling motion toward where the cancer was in his body), so you need to promise me this: no matter what happens, you go on your trips, and you stay there. There is no way I want you to cancel any of this for me. If you want me to be happy, know that I am happy that you are travelling and enjoying life. Knowing how well you are doing is what makes this all work better for me." And so, I made that promise. It felt like the right thing to do, though I've found that promises made in moments where things are going well can be challenging to keep as situations change.

In September, Kate and I went to Quebec and had a glorious time. We saw beautiful old buildings, walked on cobblestone streets, and even went for lunch in a pub that was over four hundred years old. I would phone Dad every few days and tell him what I was seeing and how beautiful it all was. It had now been nine months since Dad was given three to six months to live, so every day was a gift.

One day in Montreal, Kate and I set out to explore the Notre-Dame Basilica. We were trying to explain where we wanted to go using what little French we could remember from school to a lovely bus driver who spoke about as much English as we did French. He told us what stop to get off at and where to go after that, and we were surprised by how near to us it was—we thought the basilica was a lot farther away. As it turned out, he was directing us to the St. Catherine of Sienna Parish, and while it was not where we were originally heading, it felt as though it was where we were meant to be. Dad's mom, my Nana Perry, was named Catherine, and Dad was raised Catholic. It felt fortuitous to me, like a bit of a full-circle moment.

We went into that beautiful old church, and I found several little stations for lighting candles and saying prayers. I found one for healing, lit it, and said a prayer for my dad. Then I took a picture of the candle and the church and sent that to him. I'm not sure I know exactly how we ended up in that church, and I had never lit a candle for anyone before. All I can say is that it felt lovely, almost sacred, and I was grateful for being lost that day.

When we came back home, I went to visit Dad. We laughed and talked about the time he had gone to meet Auntie Marg in Quebec. We talked about the four-hundred-year-old pub and how he'd had lunch and a beer in that very same pub many years ago. At one point, I was telling him about how I had long ago learned how to say in French, "Please be patient with me, I speak very little French"—it was a phrase that had been very helpful on our trip. Dad asked me to say it to him in French, then he asked me to repeat it. When I did, he smiled, eyes welling with tears, and said, "I heard you the first time; I just wanted to hear you say it again." I loved that moment! Even as I type, I am holding back tears, and I can see his face and his smile. Oh, how I miss him.

Time went along and Dad continued to decline, but it just kept feeling like maybe he would somehow be okay. No one can really give anyone an exact time for their death, right? But then two days before Dave and I were supposed to leave for Hawaii, Dad took a turn for the worse and was rushed to hospice. I was devastated. It is one thing to promise someone you will go on a trip no matter what; it is a very different thing to actually go when it happens. I went over to the mainland to visit him, and he was so weak. Jamie, Dad, and I were sitting together and talking about this trip, and the whole time I was thinking, *I can't go.*

Dad said he really wanted one more Christmas—it was early November, so that didn't seem likely. Then, Jamie came up with a great idea to have a Christmas dinner together there, at hospice. He said, "Dad, if you wait for Alison to come home from Hawaii, we will have a Christmas dinner here the weekend she comes back." We all agreed.

Dave and I left on our trip, but I stayed in contact as much as I could. Jamie was amazing; he helped organize it so that I could chat with Dad. One day, though, Jamie had to make the very difficult call to let me know that Dad likely wouldn't make it through the day. He put the phone on speaker and held it so that I could chat with Dad. In fact, Jamie called every one of us kids in all our scattered locations to make sure we had an opportunity to talk with him so that nothing would be left unsaid, and he did this all while recording a new CD and planning a tour of concerts in Italy.

Thankfully, Dad rallied. There were at least four more times while I was away where all the nurses and doctors thought he would not make it through the day, and then he would make a comeback. We all had long, long talks with him, and he made sure he told all his kids what we meant to him. And yes, when Dave and I got home from Hawaii, we had Christmas dinner. Lilac and Jamie made the food at their place, and we all gathered round Dad's bed for a meal. And then he actually lived to see Christmas as well, so Dad got to have two Christmas dinners with family that year. His favourite day with his favourite people, twice—a double blessing!

As I sit here, I wonder how I will ever put into words the beauty and love we all shared in those last weeks and months. What parts of that sacred space do I even want to share? If I could have dreamed my most favourite dream and wished my most favourite wish, I would have asked for those last moments, hours, days, weeks, and months that I had, we had, with our dad.

Once Dad went into hospice, we all gathered around him and each other, and that is such a huge part of all of this. Brothers and sisters, nieces and nephews, kids and grandbabies were all gathering and loving on each other. It was so wonderful to spend time together and get to know each other again. Our brother Mike and sister-in-law Jennifer were there every day, pouring love into Dad and the entire situation. I hadn't spent a lot of time with them before, and it was such a gift to really get to know them through this time. It was wonderful to walk into the room and see Byron or Donnie playing crib with Dad. John FaceTimed with Dad one day and played his harmonica while their dog Obi howled along with him and we all laughed. This was all Dad had ever hoped for—all his kids, his family, being brought together. His death brought so much life!

Dad and I continued to laugh, talk, play cards, and tell each other about all the things we had done and not been able to share with each other over the years. One day, out of nowhere, he said to me, "You should have known every day of your life how much I loved you. I should have made sure you knew that, and I didn't. I took that from you. My own fear and selfishness took that from you. You were the love of my life, and I should have made sure you knew it. Your life would have been so different if you knew how deeply you were loved. I am so sorry."

I knew he was right. He had nine loves of his life—each of his children—and he so regretted that he had not found a way to make sure we knew that every single day, although he was sure making up for it now.

During one of the times when the hospice staff thought he wouldn't make it through the day, he got Sandy to call each of us kids so he could say goodbye. When we talked, he said that he loved me, and that he was so grateful for our time together. He thanked me for everything, and then he was fading a bit. I said, "Dad, are you okay? I'm not sure what you are saying. Is there something you need to tell me?"

Dad replied, "Yes, I need to tell you something. I need to tell you I love you two million times, and when I am finished with that, I need to tell you two million more."

"A man who has been in another world does not come back unchanged."

— C. S. Lewis

As he approached the end of his life, Dad started to have visitations—that's the only way I can describe what he shared with us. Sometimes it would be his mom and dad. Sometimes, he said it was like there was a line that went right through the middle of the room. On one side was the here and now as we could both see it, and on the other side was where he was going. He told me that there was a veil between the two that moved almost as if it were made of fluid or smoke, and he could see what was on the other side.

"I had no idea it would be like this," he told me. "I couldn't have imagined that I would be sitting here talking to you and seeing both sides."

The staff at the hospice often told us that Dad's experience was quite unique, and that it was rare for a person on so many pain medications to be so lucid. And yet there we were, discussing this incredible experience he was having.

I asked him once, "Dad, this smoky veil thing that you see, is that a something or a someone?" Dad looked kind of puzzled for a moment, then said "Oh, it's a something. Trust me, if it was a someone coming to take me away from you, I would be screaming right now!" I found that kind of funny and somewhat calming.

Dad had never had any use for religion of any sort—he had grown up Catholic but had long since left that behind. So, you can imagine our surprise when he started to have visitations from someone who he said was Jesus. The amazing thing to me, beyond the fact that my dad was telling me about these incredible experiences he was having, is that he didn't just suddenly decide, "Oh wonderful, Jesus is here." Just like everything else Dad ever looked at, he questioned what he was experiencing and his feelings about it. He told me, "I have been full of crap my entire life, and so now, just because Jesus shows up, that doesn't change that. I still need to figure out if I actually want anything to do with him, or if I am just wanting him to be here because of the situation I am in."

Imagine that. Ninety years old and literally in the last days of his life, and when Jesus himself shows up, Dad is wondering not if Jesus is actually there, but whether he wants anything to do with him. He did not want to make a decision based on fear, and it made me respect him even more.

One day, while we were chatting, Dad said to me, "I see the clock on the wall, and I know that the clock is real. And when Jesus comes to me and we talk, he is just as real as that clock. When he first started visiting me in here, I didn't want anything to do with him. Most of my life, I haven't wanted anything to do with him. And when he was coming, I just wanted to run away from him. I didn't want anything to do with him." His eyes filled with tears. "But he has taken me to a place, and there is so much love there—a love I have never known. Now, when all of a sudden I am back in this room, I am terrified and I just want to get back to him. I want to be with Jesus, with that love."

There are many ideas about what Dad was experiencing in those weeks before he passed over to the "other side," as he put it. What I believe is that he had an incredible experience with a comforter, a kindness, a forgiveness, a wave of love. Whether you believe that it was Jesus or a spirit or whatever else, I know in my heart that love completely surrounded him and took him to the very core of itself, and that he was at peace.

Dad died on January 16, 2020. A few more weeks and the COVID-19 pandemic would have made our visits impossible. We were among the very blessed to have been able to see him daily; my heart breaks for those who do not have that option.

There is so much about this experience that was so far beyond my wildest dreams. I literally would never have even dreamed that Dad and I would wade through layer after layer after layer of pain, heartbreak, abandonment, would-haves, could-haves, and should-haves to find something so beautiful. My only regret is not having sixty more years to share with this amazing man and get to know him more. Moments like these are just some of the reasons to keep pulling back the layers of trauma and pain to get to the layers of healing. Forgiveness may seem a long way off, but when it comes, it is glorious and beyond our wildest dreams.

However, that is not the end of this story.

There are many ideas about what Dad was experiencing in those weeks before he passed over to the "other side," as he put it. What I believe is that he had an incredible experience with a comforter, a kindness, a forgiveness, a wave of love.

December 6, 2020 would have been Dad's ninety-first birthday. I was soaking in a very hot tub with Epsom salts, feeling a little sad and pretty blessed, and I was missing him. My mind drifted off to imagine where he was now. Was he singing in an angelic choir? Dancing on streets of gold? Did he come back as a soon-to-be quarterback? Did he know how much I missed him? Wherever he was, I hoped he was well.

And then, it happened. My mind's eye opened wide, and there he was. Dad looked healthy and maybe a bit younger. There was music playing—beautiful, bold jubilation music, the likes of which I have only ever seen on TV in one of those southern Black Baptist churches. It was like old gospel meets Mardi Gras. He was singing and dancing, and then he turned and looked right at me. Words might fail me, but I will do my best to describe what I saw.

In his eyes was the kind of joy someone has when seeing their newborn baby for the first time. It was the joy of a groom watching his bride walk down the aisle, of a kid at Disneyland, of my grandchildren Hannah and Kashus when we took them to their first Blue Jays game at the SkyDome in Toronto, or all the kids on all the Christmas mornings—yes, those kind of twinkling eyes.

I had never heard the song he was dancing to, yet as soon as I imagined where the music might go next, it did. As I thought of lyrics, they appeared and were joyous and harmonic. I knew that in this very moment, I was somehow co-creating with heaven—a gift for me to record or perhaps a future project. I didn't know exactly what this music was, but what I did know was that Dad's joy was unspeakable and full of glory. He looked at me and said, "Don't you worry about me, sweetie!" And I realized he was still celebrating from the moment he had arrived—it was one long, continuous, glorious welcome home party. He somehow shared with me that this was, for him, all part of the first day he arrived in this glorious, love-filled place—heaven, I imagined.

I got up and grabbed my phone and began singing the song into my voice recorder, saying where the horn shots went and where the choir came in. I was orchestrating some amazing hallelujah heavenly-hosts-type jubilee, and it was freeing. I felt so alive. I am looking forward to recording this song on an upcoming CD that my brother Jamie is producing. I know that Dad would love that so much.

I was so happy and so grateful to Dad for the visit, and for all of us being so incredibly courageous in making certain that we all were able to heal and have beautiful memories of him before he left.

Thanks, Dad.

Conclusion

I am writing this book in the middle of the COVID-19 pandemic. I had carried this book inside of me for a few years and actually began writing it in early March of 2020, just after my dad passed away. I felt ready, I thought, to speak about much of my experiences with the impact of trauma throughout life, and more importantly, about the ways I have found healing. Although I do not use the words "cured" or "healed completely," I have had many years of living a life quite free from all that had haunted me for so long. Little did I know that this theory was about to be tested in a way I could not have imagined.

All around the globe, we are experiencing a shared trauma. The long-term effects are, of course, yet to be seen, but what we do see right now is how people are dealing with it all. Some were already doing their best to cope with a past trauma and now have another wrench thrown into the mix. Others may have never really had to deal with a lack of control over events in their life, and they don't have any skills available to help them cope.

We see all of this in the responses and reactions of people, especially on social media. There are unhealed traumas raging against all that is happening in our world today. There are indignant responses of the privileged who have never known this feeling of powerlessness. There are wonderful people, frightened people, confused people, angry people. We have slipped into a reality where we are somehow nouns, verbs, and adjectives all at once.

Imagine the energetic push that is happening right now. Not only is the entire planet dealing with a pandemic—the world has experienced that before—but there is also social media and Google and information and misinformation, each tap of our keys confirming our fears and stoking our anger. Some would describe this as an energy, some as something spiritual, some an evil plan; I would say that there is a movement beyond the pandemic that is travelling around the earth like a tornado, leaving rubble at every opportunity.

Whatever our views are on the pandemic itself, fear, in my way of thinking, is the force that threatens us most. I'm not talking about being afraid the pandemic is a hoax, worrying that you or someone you love will become ill, trying to determine whether or not to wear masks or social distance, vaccine or no vaccine or any of that. I'm talking about the fear that squeezes our breath from our body. Fear that has us spinning in an unrelenting loop of intrusive thoughts. Fear that has us accusing one another of a multitude of things, from being asleep to being part of it to not paying attention to not caring about the health of others and the list goes on. Fear that, once inside us, creates a world that is very difficult to navigate.

I would say that we all likely understand, to some degree, the all-encompassing nature of trauma now more than ever. Everything I have learned, both through my work and through my own experiences around trauma, has taught me that a creative release brings space to breathe and find a more peaceful existence. I am laughing to myself right now as I imagine a few people—people I adore, people so close to me—who might be thinking, are you kidding me? With all that is happening in the world, you want me to what, paint? Meditate? Sing a song? Write a poem? What are you talking about? And I am going to say yes to any and all of it. Now is possibly the most important time to find a way to express whatever is happening inside of us. If you are feeling fear and anger, maybe try journaling about that. Step away from your scrolling and researching and other ways of either numbing your mind or fuelling your fires and write. Write about how angry you are and what you might be concerned about in your own words, not someone else's. Write about it, then go for a walk and let creation take you to a place where some peace can come in, even just for a moment.

I want to put out an invitation of sorts to write until you feel too tired to write about your anger and your feelings start to spill across the page. Grab a crayon or a paint brush and scribble like an angry child for a while if that allows some of what is bubbling over to find release. Or, find some other way to be creative. Bake a cake or some cookies. Plant a garden, tend to it, and watch it grow. Build a model or organize a closet; maybe downsize and clear clutter. Finding ways to participate in creating something opens up so many possibilities.

Think of it as an experiment. Perhaps for fifteen to thirty minutes a day for seven days, try writing down how you feel—not what you think, how you feel—about anything at all and see if it relieves some pressures for you. There are many free relaxation and calming meditations available online, so another experiment might be trying one of those every day for seven days. Or hey, maybe go wild and try both. You are worth it.

In my family, music and art have always been a refuge. I have so many wonderful memories of us all singing together at Christmas or while sitting around a campfire. I have brothers who sing, brothers who build with their hands, brothers who have a hunger and thirst for knowledge and brothers who write stories and scripts. My sister is an amazing artist, as are some of my nieces. Another brother and his wife restore furniture and another brother and his wife love woodwork and art and have dedicated their lives to bringing healing to others. Our son plays sports and coaches our granddaughter, who is an amazing athlete who plays fast pitch. Our grandson is studying Tae Kwon Do and doing fabulously. Our daughter-in-law is a wonderful baker who creates beautiful cakes. Our daughter loves to walk and dance and sing and paint rocks and love on her cats Misty and Minker—her furbabies, as she calls them. I have nieces who knit and crochet and a nephew who is a rapper and a fishing guide. One nephew is a wonderful visual artist and also a rather fabulous self-taught chef. One niece loves to decorate her home and yard for every occasion, and our stepmom is an amazing interior decorator. Another niece goes hiking at every opportunity, another is the illustrator for our upcoming children's books, and another is my little nudey, fruity, yoga-loving, raw food eating, dessert wizard who is off travelling the world. We also have wonderful family in Ontario that we miss every day. There is so much I want to say and don't want to leave one thing out about these incredible people who I hold so closely in my heart.

I love my family so much that I could fill page after page with stories about how marvelous and magical they are. What I mostly want to share is that whenever we have drifted apart, we found our way back to each other. We found ways to heal and love and not just to accept our differences but celebrate them. Celebrate and find love, peace, balance, and joy, so much joy. Believe in joy. Thrive in joy!

The Art of Healing Trauma is about finding all the ways to bring balance and joy into our lives and to thrive in a world that suggests surviving is enough. There is so much creativity in you just waiting to explore all that is possible in this great, big, beautiful world. It's time to let it out!

As for me, I have spent years searching for ways of being that would bring peace to me and to those around me. Now, my studies are taking me deeper into understanding the science behind how trauma impacts our bodies and how creativity can bring healing. I've studied for years about minds, emotions, and spiritual impacts, and this is a beautiful way to bring it all together. I have created online programs to facilitate exploring all types of creativity and relaxation techniques, and I will be sharing those through my website and Facebook page soon.

Wherever you are and whatever you are experiencing, please remember to keep creating; it is a beautiful pathway to love. And remember that no matter how far down we feel we have fallen, we can always rise again.

We will rise

BY ALISON PERRY-DAVIES

We will rise
Stronger and wiser
Braver and more prepared
Kinder and more considerate

We will rise
Less concerned about what we have personally
Focussing on what we can do together
To be better

We will rise
After wondering if we ever will
After sleepless nights
After longing for connection

We will rise
Above our self-absorption
Feeling satisfied with less
Knowing ourselves more honestly

We will rise
After the kicking and screaming
After the name calling
After the blaming and finger pointing

We will rise
After our moment as sheep
When the conspiracy theories have quieted
When we remember to listen

We will rise
When we remember to celebrate each other
When we value community and love above being right
When we stop accusing and ridiculing

We will rise
When we see each other as equal
When we stop standing in our egos accusing others of slumbering
When we become cheerleaders rather than bullies

We will rise
When our moments together are seen as precious
When we remember how to be self-sufficient
When the earth is cherished and not devoured

We will rise
When we recognize the glory in creation
In our planet
In each other and ourselves

We will rise
When little girls dance while their father and brothers play on
When celebrities become people to us again
When creativity pours from dry wells

We will rise
When our songs ring out
In every voice and tongue
In every laughter and tear

We will rise
As we relearn ways of old
When we learn to long for our elders and their wisdom
When we rediscover sacred paths

We will rise
As we feel dirt in our hands planting gardens
As we deliver wine ninja gifts to friends
As we get lost in conversations with each other

We will rise
As we recognize the not so pretty sides of ourselves
As we struggle to find sense in it all
As we care for ourselves and others through this time

We will rise
Bit by bit
Piece by piece
Moment by moment

We will rise
Wondering how we ever lasted the way we used to be
Surprised by how short the time really was to get here
Grateful for fresh mercies and hope

We will rise
Changed and new
Reorganized and rejuvenated
With a perspective not previously held

We will rise
Full of understanding
Reminded that history is now
To those who will come after us

We will rise
With less answers and more questions
With a willingness to truly stop and pay attention
With an ability to quiet the rebuttals in our minds as others speak

We will rise
When we understand truly the words of Solomon Burke
Knowing deeply that none of us are free
Not when even one of us is chained

We will rise
When the grief of others is something we are willing to carry
When the lack so many experience creates hunger in our hearts
When a wrong against one feels personal to all

We will rise
As we learn to respect the right to opposing ideas
As we find ways to protect those who cannot do that for themselves
As we give space for new ways that we do not yet understand

We will rise
In the handmade greeting cards delivered to care homes
In the baked goods shared with friends
In the Zoom happy hours keeping us connected

We will rise
In the social distance walks
In the across-the-fence talks
In game nights when the TV is off

We will rise
After binge watching on Netflix
After rearranging furniture, yet again
After learning new recipes and languages and instruments

We will rise
After projects
After collaborations
After remembering how to dream

We will rise
Realizing that being together, is better
Realizing that if it isn't, maybe we need some help to change that
Realizing that family and community are important resources and supports

We will rise
After 7 p.m. thank yous
Banging pots and honking horns
Our hearts full of appreciation and feeling united

We will rise
With some uncertainty
With some goals and plans and dreams
With new understanding for what is truly important

We will rise
Remembering the beauty in a sunrise
The delight in a moment
The purity in honouring

We will rise
Beyond illusions
Beyond entitlement
Beyond insecurities

We will rise
Able
Content
Intentional

We will rise
Standing
Soaring
Strong

We will rise
Having hope.for tomorrow
Making the decision to move forward
Finding our way through

We will rise
A new day is coming
Hold fast
Stay true
We will rise
We will rise
We will rise

Phoenix Rising by Francis Dick

About the Author

Ali has been using art as part of her healing journey—both personally and professionally—for over forty years. She has been writing songs, poems, and stories and is a best-selling author. She has embraced painting and photography as avenues to release trauma and bring hope.

Ali is trained in several counselling modalities including the humanistic approach, basic counselling skills, and Elijah House training. She has diplomas in both theology and ministry and worked in ministry for over twenty years. Ali also earned an advanced diploma in human resource management as well as a diploma in holistic integrated creative arts therapy. As a lifelong learner, Ali has found many ways to facilitate communication and healing.

Ali worked as a disability case manager for the British Columbia Aboriginal Network on Disabilities Society where she learned so much from the beautiful culture and traumatic history of Indigenous people in Canada and around the world.

Ali has many years experience as a volunteer for a variety of nonprofit organizations and is certified in nonviolent crisis intervention, suicide prevention, and as a Lifeline phone counsellor for crisis intervention.

She has sat on the boards for Esquimalt and Aldergrove Military Family Resource Centres and the National Board for Military Family Resource Support serving as chairperson, secretary, and public relations, and she was a board member for Family Support Institute of British Columbia and the National Board for Visitable Housing.

Ali lives a life poured out into building healthy relationships in families, organizations, and the communities she serves in.